A
PLANTSMAN'S GUIDE TO
DAHLIAS

PHILIP DAMP

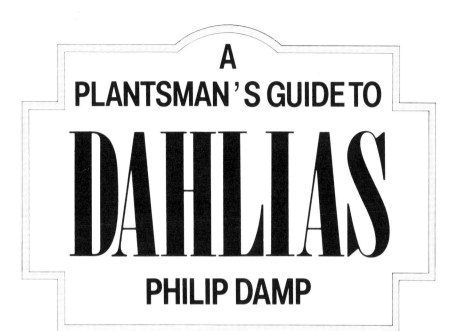

A PLANTSMAN'S GUIDE TO

DAHLIAS

PHILIP DAMP

SERIES EDITOR
ALAN TOOGOOD

WARD LOCK

© Ward Lock Ltd 1989

First published in Great Britain in 1989
by Ward Lock Limited, 8 Clifford Street
London W1X 1RB, a Cassell Company

House editor Denis Ingram

Text set by Dorchester Typesetting

Printed and bound in Great Britain by
BPCC Hazell Books Ltd
Member of BPCC Ltd
Aylesbury, Bucks, England

British Library Cataloguing in Publication Data

Damp, Philip
    A plantsman's guide to dahlias.
    1. Gardens. Dahlias. Cultivation
    I. Title.   II. Series
    635.9'3355

ISBN 0-7063-6740-5

CONTENTS

PUBLISHER'S NOTE

Readers are requested to note that in order to make the text intelligible in both hemispheres, plant flowering times, etc. are described in terms of seasons, not months. The following table provides an approximate 'translation' of seasons into months for the two hemispheres.

Northern Hemisphere		Southern Hemisphere
Mid-winter	= January	= Mid-summer
Late winter	= February	= Late summer
Early spring	= March	= Early autumn
Mid-spring	= April	= Mid-autumn
Late spring	= May	= Late autumn
Early summer	= June	= Early winter
Mid-summer	= July	= Mid-winter
Late summer	= August	= Late winter
Early autumn	= September	= Early spring
Mid-autumn	= October	= Mid-spring
Late autumn	= November	= Late spring
Early winter	= December	= Early summer

Captions for colour photographs on chapter-opening pages:

Pp. 12–13 'Mignon' seeds can be relied on to yield a superb mixture of rich-coloured single blooms on dwarf plants, fine for beds and borders.

Pp. 20–21 A fine mixture of Cactus and Decorative dahlias forming a border display against a backcloth of golden conifers in a Scottish park.

Pp. 28–29 A group of cut flower dahlias in Cactus, Semi-cactus, Ball and Decorative form, illustrating the wide colour range.

Pp. 64–65 A typical dahlia border filled with a range of varieties, from dwarfs to giants in a mixture of colours and flower shapes to give an unbroken display from mid-summer to mid-autumn.

Pp. 92–93 A well grown dahlia garden in high summer is a wonderful sight. Better still, you can cut from this display for your home and never miss the blooms!

Pp. 108–9 'Miyako Bijin', perhaps one of the best of the recent Japanese arrivals. Its startling colour would make it wanted anywhere, as a Medium Cactus for exhibition or garden enhancement.

Pp. 116–7 'Princess Marie Jose', a single-flowered bedding variety, is a delightful luminous lilac pink that also makes excellent cut blooms.

EDITOR'S FOREWORD

This unique series takes a completely fresh look at the most popular garden and greenhouse plants.

Written by a team of leading specialists, yet suitable for novice and more experienced gardener alike, the series considers modern uses of the plants, including refreshing ideas for combining them with other garden or greenhouse plants. This should appeal to the more general gardener who, unlike the specialist, does not want to devote a large part of the garden to a particular plant. Many of the planting schemes and modern uses are beautifully illustrated in colour.

The extensive A-Z lists describe in great detail hundreds of the best varieties and species available today.

For the historically-minded, each book opens with a brief history of the subject up to the present day and, as appropriate, looks at the developments by plant breeders.

The books cover all you need to know about growing and propagating. The former embraces such aspects as suitable sites and soils, planting methods, all-year-round care and how to combat pests, diseases and disorders.

Propagation includes raising plants from seeds and by vegetative means, as appropriate.

For each subject there is a society (sometimes more), full details of which round off each book.

The plants that make up this series are very popular and examples can be found in many gardens. However, it is hoped that these books will encourage gardeners to try some of the better, or perhaps more unusual, varieties; ensure some stunning plant associations; and result in the plants being grown well.

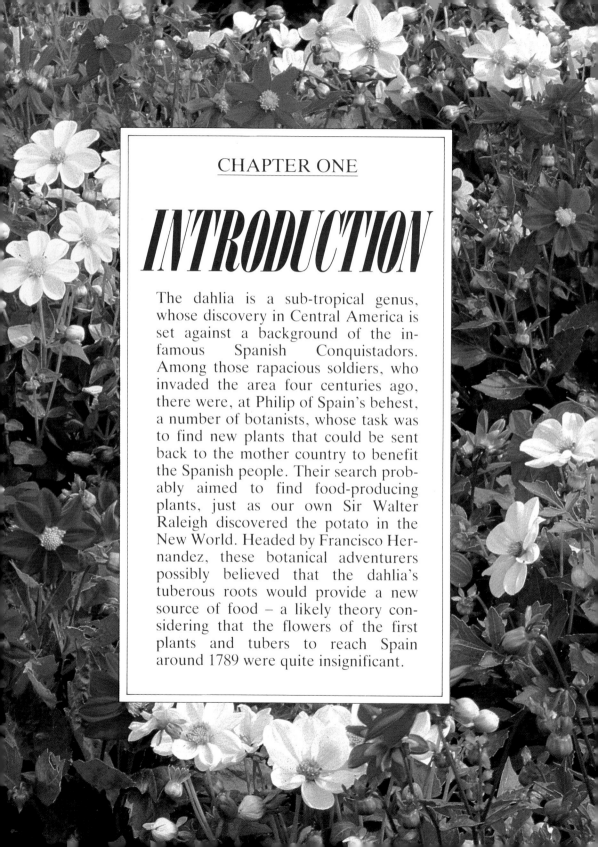

CHAPTER ONE

INTRODUCTION

The dahlia is a sub-tropical genus, whose discovery in Central America is set against a background of the infamous Spanish Conquistadors. Among those rapacious soldiers, who invaded the area four centuries ago, there were, at Philip of Spain's behest, a number of botanists, whose task was to find new plants that could be sent back to the mother country to benefit the Spanish people. Their search probably aimed to find food-producing plants, just as our own Sir Walter Raleigh discovered the potato in the New World. Headed by Francisco Hernandez, these botanical adventurers possibly believed that the dahlia's tuberous roots would provide a new source of food – a likely theory considering that the flowers of the first plants and tubers to reach Spain around 1789 were quite insignificant.

ARRIVAL IN EUROPE

The first shipments were sent to Abbé Cavanilles, then curator of the Botanical Gardens in Madrid. He grew these sub-tropical plants from a world he had never seen nor was ever likely to see, but lost them all through over-culture! Later supplies, however, experienced a better fate, it is recorded. Searching for a name for this unlikely import from the Americas, the good Abbot decided to give the plant the name of a close friend he had worked with, a Swedish gentleman and student of the famous Linnaeus, named Andreas Dahl. So this Mexican immigrant became the dahlia, and the early varieties raised from the seeds and roots that had come tossing across the South Atlantic to the Spanish seaports were given such names as *D. coccinea*, *D. merckii* and, most descriptive of all, *D. variabilis*.

But the name Dahlia was not acceptable to all of Europe's independent horticulturists. Some considered the newcomer would be confused with the day lily. Others decided, after experimenting with the new arrival, that it should be called Georgina, in honour of Professor Georgi, a Russian horticulturist. The name Georgina stuck for generations and though Dahlia is now used all over the world, Georginas are still referred to in Northern Europe, especially in Sweden and parts of Russia.

Despite, or perhaps because of, the dahlia's puny beginnings, nurserymen and growers handling the new plants looked for every possible way of improving them. They soon found that the dahlia is a natural hybridizer. A batch of seeds from one plant will yield progeny distinctly different from their parent – almost always in colour and quite often in form too. Such exciting potential created a furore in the main participating countries – France, England and Germany. The Spanish, it seems, had little interest in the flower once the first excitement passed, so the scene shifted dramatically to other countries.

The French experimented with the possibility of producing food from the prolific dahlia, but the tubers proved not to be to the taste of this nation of gourmets. They then fed the roots to their livestock, but these too found them unpalatable. The English, however, with their reputation as mercenary traders – Napoleon called us a nation of shopkeepers, remember? – decided that the dahlia could became a commercial proposition and set about creating a whole new range of forms and colours.

GLOBE DAHLIAS

These were headed by the inevitable double-flowered type with a completely globular bloom. First called the globe dahlia, it later became the all-conquering Double Show and Fancy dahlia – Double signifying double-flowered, Show of a single colour and Fancy a mixture of several colours.

This type dominated our Victorian forebears' floral thinking. By the mid-nineteenth century over 10,000 Double Show and Fancy varieties had been catalogued and new ones from the finest nurseries commanded as much as £100 for a single tuber. Every colour had been found, except the elusive blue. You could have lilacs, lavenders and mauves by the thousand, but no blue. The search for a blue dahlia reached such exciting proportions that a London newspaper offered £1,000 – a sizeable fortune in those days – for the first grower, amateur or professional, who could raise one. The money was never claimed and even today no dahlia boasts that legendary sky-blue colouring.

Scientists tell us that the original hybrids that came to Europe lacked the necessary pigment to give a blue flower. Many have optimistically named their introductions 'Blue Moon', 'Boy Blue', 'Bonny Blue' or even 'Nearest Blue', a Dutch offering that summarizes the situation, but neither the Royal Horticultural Society nor the National Dahlia Society, the senior authorities for administering the dahlia in this country, have ever classified a variety as blue, or even listed blue in their colour groupings!

But if blue was not possible, all the other colours of the rainbow certainly were. Brilliant scarlets, yellows as soft as the morning sky or as bright as butter abounded. Add to this range many suffusions (overlaid colours), blends, tipped (bicolor) varieties, those striped along the length of their petals and others whose basic colour was splashed or dotted with another.

NEW SHAPES

By the 1870s nurserymen were starting to appreciate the dahlia's ability to mutate, and various European hybrid-

ists were able to give us new petal formations. The Germans gave us a miniature version of the Double Show and Fancy which we know today as the Pompon dahlia, while the French presented a fascinated gardening world with the lovely Collerette – spelt like the French word with an 'e' rather than an 'a'. These were open-centred blooms with an inner ring of petals shorter than the outer ones and often of a contrasting colour – hence Collerette. The Dutch, who eventually emerged as masters of the commercial dahlia, gave us a dramatically new form in the 1870s which became known as the Cactus dahlia since its tight, rolled petals resembled those of desert cacti.

At home, our own hybridists were not averse to importing these new forms and either selling them to their customers or using them to produce new varieties and even new forms. One such arrival was the so-called Paeony-flowered dahlia with broad, strap-like petals, which has persisted until recently in the National Dahlia Society's classification lists. This form gave way around the turn of the century to the popular Decorative dahlia with its broad, flat petals that reflex towards the rear of the bloom and occasionally have slightly incurved margins. Other forms have emerged from this, like the Waterlily dahlias, a recent group given official status by the N.D.S. They resemble the flowers after which they are named, as do the Carnation-flowered types with split petal tips, just like our favourite wedding flowers.

Many other forms have arisen, some to stay for a while and then disappear,

others to intrigue and puzzle those whose job it is to classify them. To cover this quirk of the dahlia, the National Dahlia Society has created a convenient pigeonhole labelled Miscellaneous. Into this can go anything that arises. It currently contains, for instance, the single and double-flowered Orchid dahlias, which resemble their namesakes. There will soon be others like the Chrysanthemum-flowered types, some of which are now arriving from the Far East, and the startling Star dahlias that have five or six petals radiating from a bright yellow centre.

DAHLIA SOCIETY FORMED

To cope with the rising enthusiasm for this chameleon among ornamentals the National Dahlia Society was formed in London in 1881. At first it was really a gentleman's club whose members competed against each other to see who could create the finest blooms. (Or rather, their gardeners competed for them, because in the late Victorian era not many folk had gardens where flowers could be grown to perfection, the cash to buy the plants or tubers and the wherewithal to transport them to the many special dahlia shows that were springing up.)

A further 25 years elapsed before a brave President of the National Dahlia Society, Edward Mawley, wrote passionately in its journal that the Society

'Princess Marie Jose' makes larger blooms than the Coltness strain on taller plants, but is a superb bedder and also good for cutting.

should strive to popularize the dahlia and extend its range. From then on the Society's new generous outlook aroused a spreading demand for dahlias for all the flower gardener's summer needs. Hybridists consequently turned away from the strict conventional lines of the exhibition dahlia – though such blooms remain firm favourites – to produce dahlias suitable for bedding and park decoration, strong growers to yield cut blooms for market or to fill vases at home, and delicately constructed blooms to take the eye of the flower arrangers.

Dahlias for all these purposes are now freely available, of course, but at times the Society struggled to establish itself. The years between the two World Wars saw many more ordinary folk with their own small gardens and the dahlia became a strong contender to form part of their summer display. Yet the Society's membership rose very slowly. Few people wanted to spend money in the twenties and thirties to join a flower society, so, when the Second World War ended there were a mere 500 members on the Society's books.

Suddenly, though, things changed as people became keen on exhibiting. Showmen had earlier been asked to stage from 12 to 24 vases of dahlias, but the calls were now much smaller, so everyone could manage to show. Transport became easier too and the reasonable-sized gardens on new housing estates enabled dahlia enthusiasts to provide for their families from their vegetable plots and still raise some show blooms. As the late forties opened into the fifties, the National Dahlia Society's membership rose dramatically from 500 to 2,000, then 4,000. When I took over as Secretary in 1967 the highest ever membership of 7,300 had been reached.

The rising tide of gardening societies had made much of this possible, as their members insisted that dahlia classes should be included in the schedules for their annual shows. This created a need for dahlia judges, which the N.D.S. undertook to provide – and still does. Specialist nurseries sprang into being and the Continentals showered the market with dahlia novelties from all over the world at prices most could easily afford. Gardening magazines catered for the needs of dahlia lovers. If they did not, their readership fell sharply, especially as other leading flowers like roses, chrysanthemums, gladioli and sweet peas were undergoing similar development. So the dahlia had become popular, as Ted Mawley had predicted, and made a place for itself in the hearts and minds of British gardeners.

DAHLIAS TODAY

Today we can look at the dahlia with pride. Here in Britain we have the world's largest dahlia society – twice the size of its nearest challenger in the United States. The finest dahlia show in the world is held every year in the Royal Horticultural Society's New Hall in Westminster, London, and the second best show in conjunction with the Great Autumn Show in Harrogate, North Yorkshire. The world's most prestigious dahlia trials are held in Wisley Gardens,

Surrey, home of the R.H.S., and jointly administered by that body and the National Dahlia Society. Awards made at Wisley are published in gardening journals and newspapers worldwide. The selection of a raiser's new variety for inclusion in the trials is a fiercely sought honour. Once achieved, it is cherished with pride.

Perhaps one of the greatest benefits to emerge from our national love for the dahlia is that its development is uppermost in the minds of everyone in the Society. Special classes for new dahlia cultivars are staged every year in the London and Harrogate shows and the search is always on for something better than the current types, for new and exciting forms to continue the dahlia's ongoing development, which began way back before Queen Victoria came to the throne.

If you find a spark of interest in this versatile flower, I would heartily recommend you to join the many thousands who find such pleasure in growing it in its various forms – for garden decoration, as a cut flower, for exhibition, for use in the delicate art of flower arranging and even in raising new varieties, all of which I shall be dealing with in the chapters that follow.

CHAPTER TWO

PLANTING IDEAS

Important though it is to grow your dahlias well to ensure bountiful crops of high quality blooms you can be proud of, you also need to give careful thought to where you are going to plant them and how you will arrange them if you want a display people cannot help but admire.

Of course, plants you are growing to yield top-class blooms for exhibition or armfuls of flowers to fill your summer vases can just be lined out on your vegetable plot, provided you give them all the water, food, support and protection they need. But an attention-riveting garden display depends as much on the arrangement of the plants as on how they are grown.

EFFECTIVE SITING

One of the best ways of growing dahlias for your own personal pleasure is to site your display where it can be viewed from your lounge windows.

Some displays I have helped to create have had tiered beds to give more height, but this is not essential as the dahlia provides for this quite naturally. Many modern varieties suitable for such a display easily grow 1.5–1.8 m (5–6 ft) high and can form the back row, each supported by a 'cage' of three canes, soon to be hidden by a second row of plants reaching 90 cm–1.2 m (3–4 ft) high. In front of these, hiding the second row's supports, will be a row of smaller growing varieties, 60 cm (2 ft) tall. This row could be wired for support or grown through 15 cm (6 in) square wire mesh as at Wisley, which would be hidden and not harm these lower growing plants. Then along the front of the display you could plant some bedders or patio dahlias without support. Some dahlia blooms now grow only 2.5 cm (1 in) across and cushion out to make perfect foils for the other forms.

Such a display bed has several things to commend it to the ordinary gardener. Its beauty has to be seen to be believed. Choose the right colours and you will gain the startled admiration of your family and friends as combinations of brilliant scarlets and bright golden yellows, for instance, are set off by stunning pastel shades. Some of the more flamboyant dahlias – eye-catching bi-colors, including purple-edged whites and butter yellows tipped golden orange – could be strategically placed here and there.

BEDDING VARIETIES

Dahlias provide amply for the needs of the ordinary gardener who wants to pack a flower bed with summer-long colour. This can be done quite easily with bedding dahlias. As we shall see in a later chapter, there are several types of these – some simple five-petalled kinds that can be raised from spring-sown seeds, others special named bedders raised from cuttings or by dividing their old tubers into several pieces. The advantage of planting named varieties is that you can lift the roots after a full season's display and store them over winter ready for a repeat performance the next year.

Seed-raised dahlias behave quite differently. Our seed firms have made great strides in producing dahlias that come almost true to form, like the popular Cactus, Semi-cactus and Collerette varieties, but colours can never be guaranteed. The Coltness Gem dwarf bedders illustrate this well. Raised from seed, they will give you an array of open-centred blooms, each with a row of five or six petals, the classic dwarf bedder form, but will range in colour right through the spectrum from white to purple, missing only that elusive blue.

Dwarf bedding dahlias need little or no staking, but I would recommend you to set small sticks or twigs among the plants early on. As they reach their maximum height – 30–45 cm (12–18 in) –

such unobtrusive supports will be ample to hold the plants upright. Later, they will support each other.

Like other kinds of dahlias, dwarf bedders need regular dead-heading to keep up a continuous supply of blooms. But with only a few petals to drop, a dwarf's flower can become a seedhead almost overnight and it is often difficult to distinguish a bud from a conical seedhead. It is specially difficult on the popular Topmix or Lilliput forms, whose blooms are barely 2.5 cm (1 in) across. Here particularly, with buds little larger than a pea, a seedhead can so easily be confused with a bud.

FOR FLAT DWELLERS

This assumes that you have a garden in which to create such a display. But what if you have no garden but live in a high-rise flat or a house with only a small patio at the rear? Well, there is no reason why you could not enjoy dahlias in containers instead.

One friend I visited had been a life-long dahlia lover and grower. As he grew older he sold his house and garden and moved into a flat in Ealing, London, where he had succeeded in creating the most elegant display of dahlias imaginable on the balcony of a flat three floors up. To achieve this he had built several containers carefully designed to hold his favourite types – mainly spherical Ball varieties and Pompons. He set reasonably priced growing bags inside wooden frames that could support his canes and stakes. I well recall a set of Pompon plants blooming fiercely at 60–90 cm (2–3 ft) high.

Then he had a collection of dwarf bedders and Topmix forms needing no support in smaller containers. His delighted wife was able to cut enough blooms from this display to keep a permanent display of dahlias in their lounge all summer.

FOR TUBS AND CONTAINERS

Just think how your own skills and ambitions could have full rein here, making suitable wooden, cement or polythene containers to hold soil – and bright-flowered dahlias. Those less inclined to DIY will find a wide choice of containers at any garden centre or nursery. If you decide on this approach, I do recommend you to go for the deepest containers you can find. Troughs or tubs that can take 30 cm (1 ft) or more of good compost would be ideal. But before putting any soil in the containers, make sure there is adequate drainage. If no drainage holes have been provided, then make some in the base at least 2.5 cm (1 in) across and some 8–10 cm (3–4 in) apart. Cover these with pieces of broken clay pot or small pebbles, then follow with the compost.

I would suggest you use a reliable brand of 'no-soil' compost, like Levington or Arthur Bower's – first class for good dahlia root growth. Being light in weight it makes it easier to move your containers too. You can easily slot thin canes or stakes down the sides in the 30 cm (12 in) deep soil, but do this while planting. If you push them in later after your plants' roots have spread, you could damage them.

When selecting varieties for a patio display, keep to those of compact habit which grow no more than 60cm (2ft) high. I have seen larger types grown successfully. (Believe me, there is no more startling sight than a couple of giant dahlias with blooms as big as footballs flowering away on a patio.) But they demand a lot of time and attention to succeed. With standard varieties of the height I have recommended, you still have a choice of some of the finest dahlias in cultivation.

I can hardly over-emphasize the importance of watering patio dahlia gardens. It would be difficult to overwater, given the good drainage I have recommended, but once the foliage has spread over and around the sides of the container, as it quickly does, rain may not penetrate, even during quite a heavy rainstorm, so water and water regularly.

COMBINING DAHLIAS WITH OTHER PLANTS

While some dahlia enthusiasts, particularly exhibitors and others who wish to produce perfect blooms, will grow their favourite flowers on their own, with no other plants nearby, there are many more general gardeners who will want to combine dahlias with some of their other plants. This is certainly true for those who want to grow only a few plants for garden display and/or cutting – and, indeed, for those who have only small gardens. Of course, dahlias do not associate aesthetically nor practically with all garden plants, so one has to be careful when planning plant associations with them. On the other hand, some groups of hardy plants make ideal companions for them.

It is necessary at the outset to provide all the cultural conditions that dahlias require and which are fully described elsewhere in this book. For example, plenty of sun is extremely important, so it would be ridiculous to plant dahlias with shade-loving plants. The plants you combine with dahlias must relish the same conditions, if such groupings are to be successful.

☐ IN THE MIXED BORDER

It is safe to say that in most gardens today plants are grown in mixed borders, which can consist of all kinds of hardy plants as well as temporary tender kinds. The main permanent 'framework' of a mixed border generally consists of hardy shrubs, of both flowering and foliage kinds. Other plants are grouped around and among them – hopefully artistically, to create some pleasing plant associations – hardy perennials and bulbs among them. A mixed border can also include hardy and half-hardy annuals, tender perennials (such as dahlias) and biennials.

Dahlias certainly look pleasing with a number of shrubs and hardy perennials. I particularly like to associate red-flowered dahlias with foliage shrubs,

Opposite: *This dahlia border shows the double benefit of a dense, rich-green foliage ground cover and a succession of colourful blooms.*

such as purple-leaved cotinus or berberis. Red dahlias also combine well with silver- or grey-leaved shrubs like *Senecio* 'Sunshine' or lavender. Yellow dahlias look good with silver or grey foliage too.

Rose-lovers are likely to include some shrub roses in a mixed border – dahlias make pleasing companions for these, especially if you choose harmonising or pleasantly contrasting colours. I would suggest red roses and red dahlias, for instance, or pink roses and pink dahlias.

Also use dahlias to take over from spring- or early summer-flowering shrubs, which often appear dull once their show is over.

Dahlias can also be used effectively with shrubs noted for autumn interest, such as foliage tints and berries, like euonymus, rhus and cotoneasters.

□ IN THE HERBACEOUS BORDER

Borders devoted purely to herbaceous perennials had their heyday in the early part of this century when large gardens, maintained by numerous gardeners, were commonplace. But interest in these plants is very strong again today, though they are now generally grown with other plants in mixed beds and borders. However, as there is also a resurgent interest in the English style of gardening, the true herbaceous border may yet make a comeback. It certainly has in my garden. A few years ago I planted a traditional herbaceous border, backed by a laurel hedge, and it gives me a great deal of pleasure. But it is completely bare in the winter, of course.

A more modern way of growing hardy perennials on their own is in informal 'island' beds set in a lawn – a superb idea pioneered by Alan Bloom of Bressingham Gardens.

Dahlias, both dwarf bedding and taller kinds, can be used to fill any gaps in herbaceous beds and borders. However well such a bed or border is planned, one always seems to end up with gaps. A plant has died, perhaps, or a group of plants has not filled out as much as expected. Of course, dahlias can be used in their own right in herbaceous beds and borders, not just as gap-fillers. Their flower display lasts longer than that of most hardy herbaceous plants.

Again, one should plan as far as possible, for dahlias do not combine well aesthetically with all hardy perennials. With their rounded, often ball-shaped blooms, dahlias contrast well with perennials with bold spikes of blooms, such as delphiniums. Red dahlias and purple delphiniums go well together and I like yellow dahlias with the traditional blue varieties of delphinium. Be sure to choose tall-growing dahlias to combine with delphiniums.

Dwarf bedding dahlias can take over from spring or early-summer flowering perennials, if planted in front of groups of hardy perennials. One perennial which looks decidedly tatty after it has flowered is the oriental poppy, *Papaver orientale*. This would certainly benefit from having its foliage hidden by a group of dwarf or medium-height dahlias planted in front of it.

Coming into autumn, dahlias are perfect companions for late-flowering herbaceous plants like perennial asters (Michaelmas daisies) and *Sedum spectabile*.

□ SINGLE-COLOUR SCHEMES

The idea of growing plants of only one colour together in beds and borders is not new. It was never widely practised, but interest in single-colour schemes is now reviving. Not long ago there was a garden-centre campaign to 'think pink'.

Some gardens open to the public have for long been noted for their single-colour beds and borders, notably Hidcote Manor Gardens in Gloucestershire. This garden is famed (among other things) for its red border. When I once visited, in summer, I greatly admired red dahlias with dark foliage growing with red roses, and purple delphiniums providing a contrast in shape.

Single-colour schemes are a thought, then, if you are tiring of the restless riot of colours in your garden. I am not suggesting that you give over the entire garden to one colour, but just parts of it. Say, the area around a patio where the colour could perhaps link with an interior colour scheme, creating a co-ordinated effect. Or parts of a bed or border could feature a single colour. Areas around the house could link up with the exterior colour of the house.

Dahlias are highly suitable for including in single-colour schemes, for they come in almost every colour.

□ SUMMER BEDDING SCHEMES

Growing dwarf bedding dahlias on their own in beds to provide a long and highly colourful summer display, which lasts into the autumn, has already been mentioned, but do not forget that other bedding plants can be combined with them to create some pleasing summer bedding schemes. There are a number of colourful ideas you can follow.

I learned the use of dwarf dahlias for bedding when I was a parks' apprentice. I will never forget the superb beds of yellow dwarf bedding dahlias interplanted with violet-flowered *Verbena venosa*, and silver-leaved *Cineraria maritima* dot plants.

We used dahlias in some sub-tropical bedding schemes too. Dwarf bedding varieties formed the main carpet, in which were scattered cannas (Indian shot) with their bold bronze or green leaves and flamboyant lily-like flowers, and standard fuchsias.

Other dot plants you could use in beds of dwarf dahlias to create height and contrast include *Abutilon striatum* 'Thompsonii' with yellow and green variegated foliage. This is a tender shrub, very popular for summer bedding schemes. Standard plants of heliotrope also make good dot plants among dahlias – especially yellow varieties. Ornamental maize (*Zea mays*) can also be recommended, especially for sub-tropical bedding schemes. The castor-oil plant, *Ricinus communis*, grown for its green or bronze foliage, combines superbly with bedding dahlias and is another suitable candidate for a sub-tropical scheme.

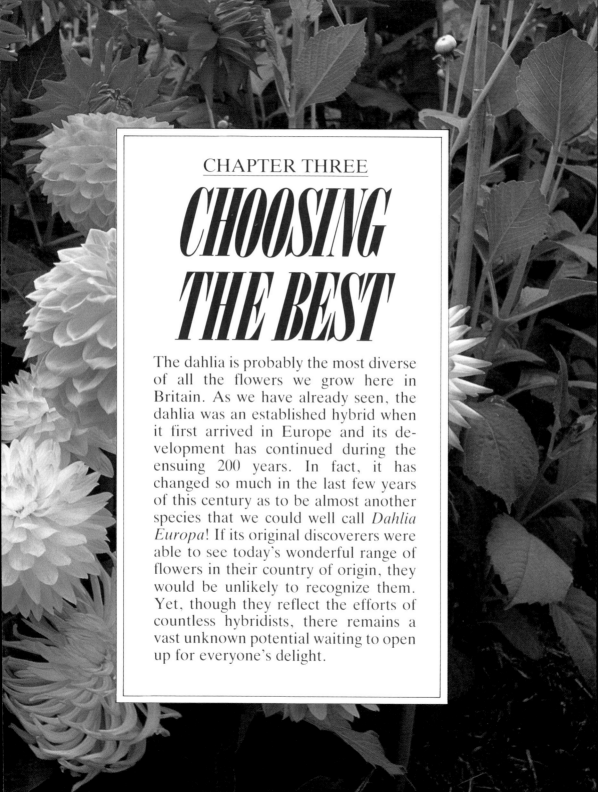

CHAPTER THREE

CHOOSING THE BEST

The dahlia is probably the most diverse of all the flowers we grow here in Britain. As we have already seen, the dahlia was an established hybrid when it first arrived in Europe and its development has continued during the ensuing 200 years. In fact, it has changed so much in the last few years of this century as to be almost another species that we could well call *Dahlia Europa*! If its original discoverers were able to see today's wonderful range of flowers in their country of origin, they would be unlikely to recognize them. Yet, though they reflect the efforts of countless hybridists, there remains a vast unknown potential waiting to open up for everyone's delight.

Currently, we are indebted to our National Dahlia Society for listing and categorizing the types we see in our gardens and nurseries. The Royal Horticultural Society, with the same objective – to bring order out of confusion – has been given the task of cataloguing every named dahlia as International Registrar, which they have been doing since they were appointed in 1966 by the International Horticultural Congress held in Maryland, U.S.A. They have produced the only International Register in existence, the so-called *Tentative Classified List and International Register of Dahlia Names*. With its several amendments, this book (first published in 1969), is unfortunately now only available from second-hand gardening booksellers.

The National Dahlia Society, by virtue of their statutes, are a little more up to date than the R.H.S. and publish a *Classified Directory* bi-annually, the latest issued in January, 1989. This lists dahlia varieties relevant to its members' needs – those for showmen, those yielding fine cut flowers and others first-rate for garden decoration. This book can be obtained from the National Dahlia Society's General Secretary, 8 Station Road, Kirby Muxloe, Leicester.

With one minor difference, both societies classify dahlias in ten separate groupings and forms, decided according to their petal formation. Each classification has its own uses, some overlapping to offer two or three. Each grouping is further sub-divided into sizes, as the richly talented dahlia can produce blooms from 5cm (2in) in diameter to 30cm (12in) across within the same grouping. Besides this, every dahlia fits into one of 13 colour classifications.

It is amazing to think that between them these groupings, sizes and colours provide several thousand separate slots into which dahlia varieties can be fitted – hence my congratulations to the R.H.S. and the N.D.S., who have for many years brought order to what could have been a hopeless chaos. Other international societies devoted to the dahlia have generally fallen into line with the British standards and use the colour divisions sponsored and administered by the R.H.S. Now let us look at some of those categories of dahlias:

Group 1. Single-flowered

These have a single, occasionally overlapping, outer ring of florets, with the centre forming a disc (eventually a seedhead). They include the seed-raised bedding varieties, sometimes known as dwarf bedding dahlias, as well as those special Single-flowered types that have been given cultivar names because of their special value. In this latter type can be included the fascinating Lilliput or Topmix dahlias that grow only 30cm (1ft) or so in height and mass their small bushy plants with blooms only 2.5cm (1in) or so in diameter. This latter group is suitable for growing in containers on a patio or balcony.

The Singles are perhaps most effectively used by professional gardeners to fill the flower beds in the nation's parks and gardens with millions of cheerful dahlias every summer.

Coltness Gem

This seed selection can be purchased quite cheaply from any garden centre and will provide you with masses of first class plants growing only 30 cm (1 ft) or so high (maybe a little more in a wet season). The blooms are single and open-centred, and the colour varied with no guarantee that any particular hue is present.

Mignon

Seed of this is widely available and will give excellent results for minor expenditure. Claimed by the originator to have 'jewel-like' colours, they are certainly very bright and grow on small plants only 35 cm (14 in) high.

'Nellie Geerlings'

This famous Dutch-raised bedding variety is a bright red Single that grows a little taller than some. Its value lies in the fact that you can block-plant with this named variety and know that your flower bed will be a mass of scarlet bloom all summer.

'Princess Marie Jose'

An elegant named Single that can be used for bedding and another that has stood the test of time. Over 40 years old, this lilac beauty has been a favourite with the Harrogate parks authority for many years. On occasion, it can also supply blooms for your vases.

Rigoletto

Yet another dwarf-growing Single-flowered seed strain, with open-centred flowers. Only 37.5 cm (15 in) high, the plants show wide variation in flower colour.

Redskin

Another seed strain, this one is noted for its coppery bronze foliage, which sets off the yellow and orange blooms beautifully. A goodly percentage of double-flowered varieties could appear, but it is still a dwarf grower whose colouring is not guaranteed.

'Yellow Hammer'

This named Single-flowered bedder, coloured as its name, has been a long and faithful servant of gardeners interested in bedding schemes. The brightest of yellows, it is a low grower which blooms consistently from early summer to late autumn. A classic variety you must buy as plants, not seed.

Group 2. Anemone-flowered

This one's blooms form one or more outer rings of flattened ray florets around a dense central group of tubular florets which fill the centre, making this a double-flowered type.

This dahlia form is rare and only a few varieties are currently in commerce. Most grow only 45-60 cm (1½-2 ft) high, and so are excellent in bedding or display schemes. In fact some have that overlap value mentioned earlier, being categorized as dwarf bedding types as well as Anemone-flowered. They are of little value as cut blooms and I have never seen them exhibited at flower shows. That is not to say that they would not make a very colourful addition to a show schedule. Their main disadvantage would be that their stems are not as robust as those of some of the other

This scarlet selection from the Coltness hybrid range is a fine rich colour, guaranteed to play a key role in some bedding schemes, as a batch of mixed colours could never do.

The Coltness hybrids have long been relied upon to yield a fine display of single flowers within a few months of seed sowing. This clear sunshine yellow has terrific impact.

forms. I have seen Anemone-flowered dahlias growing strongly in containers on a patio, providing a colourful background to other forms yet demanding very little care.

'Brio'

A low-growing type, with flame and orange flowers – a brilliant combination. This one has double blooms and is one of the few Doubles that need no canes for support. It can create a spectacular display, quite different from that the Singles give. Height 45 cm (1½ ft).

'Comet'

A taller growing Anemone dahlia, around a metre (3¼ ft) high, with scarlet blooms some 7.5–10 cm (3–4 in) in diameter. This one will provide you with some cut flowers, whose form is bound to intrigue your friends.

'Honey'

This is a mixture of colours – bronze, pink and some yellow! Another Anemone-flowered bedding type, which blends well with 'Brio' above.

'Scarlet Comet'

A lighter, brighter red sport of 'Comet', and with all the characteristics of the parent. A pity there are not more of these, they can be so charming. Height 75 cm (2½ ft).

Group 3. Collerette

If you think the word Collerette should be spelt with an 'a' rather than the 'e', then I should explain that this type originated in France around the turn of the century and so the word is in its French form. These lovely dahlias resemble the Single-flowered types, but each flower has a central 'collar' of shorter petals (hence the name), often of a contrasting colour – say a scarlet with yellow collar or a lilac with a white collar. In fact there are so many combinations that the range is endless, except for that blue we are still seeking! The height of most varieties in this group ranges from 75–90 cm (2½ to 3 ft), and the flower widths vary only slightly between 7.5 and 12.5 cm (3 and 5 in).

They can be used for most purposes, so they could truthfully be called 'dual purpose' dahlias. As cut flowers they will offer a mass of bloom from first flowering in mid-summer until the frosts, and there is no better type for floral art than the versatile Collerette, as most varieties can open from the bud stage in water. This means that an arrangement can be made with partly open dahlias and others that are fully out. Their colour range makes them a joy to grow for garden pleasure, and if you would like to enjoy this group at its best, I would recommend you to seek out the list or catalogue of some specialist nurseryman whose range is fantastic.

The Collerette also exhibits well, and in the hands of a skilled showman can make a fine addition to any show. There are even special trophy classes at our national shows for this form. While it would not be true to say that it is as popular as some of the better known exhibition types, recent years have brought this French foundling more enthusiasts than ever before.

'Chimborazo'
A typical colourful Collerette, with red outer petals and a bright golden-yellow collar. Height around 90 cm (3 ft) with plenty of blooms for cut flowers or for show work.

'Choh'
Perhaps the smallest Collerette in commerce, with rich purple outside petals, the inner ones being white. From Japan (its name means 'butterfly') with flowers only 5 cm (2 in) in diameter. A little winner, 75 cm (2½ ft) tall.

'Clair de Lune'
Of almost geometric form, quite rare in the Collerette section. As the name would suggest, its colouring is a blend of yellows, darker on the outer petals, paler on the collar. The plants reach 90 cm (3 ft) high.

'Easter Sunday'
The essential all white. With its bright golden eye, this is a truly elegant dahlia. Excellent for cut flowers or garden decoration, it makes a strong plant around 90 cm (3 ft) high.

'La Cierva'
The most popular Collerette for exhibition. Dutch raised, it is a startling purple/red tipped white with a white collar. Height around 1 metre (3¼ ft), sturdy and well formed.

'Rosalie'
This recent arrival is a combination of dark and light pinks. Ideal for exhibition, it cuts well and makes a fine addition to any floral arrangement. Plants around 90 cm (3 ft) high.

Group 4. Waterlily-flowered

The most recent group established by the National Dahlia Society, which has not yet been adopted by the Royal Horticultural Society. This is at present the only difference between the two classifications. As its name suggests, this is a 'look-alike' grouping, each bloom of Waterlily-flowered varieties being fully double (with its centre completely covered), with rather sparse florets that give the blooms a shallow appearance, much like the Queen of the garden pool it emulates. Some of the petals are straight or slightly involute along their length, giving the bloom that typically flat appearance. Plant heights are standard around 90–120 cm (3–4 ft) and, of course, need some support during the growing period. They have no equal as cut flowers, and it is among the Waterlilies that some of the legendary cut flower varieties are listed, like the Dutch-raised pink 'Gerrie Hoek', first introduced in 1946, given an Award of Merit at the famous Wisley Trials in 1949, and still a best seller grown worldwide by an army of dahlia lovers. Similarly, yellow 'Glorie van Heemstede', released in 1947, received a Highly Commended award at Wisley in 1949, and, almost 40 years on, an Award of Merit in 1986. Elegant 'Glorie' has never lost its vigour or appeal and is still a favourite with growers everywhere. It has recently come into its own as an exhibition flower, as it no longer needs to compete against the more heavily built Decorative forms.

In a separate group, it can now enter

shows competing only with other Waterlily-flowered varieties. But perhaps the best niche for these favourite dahlias is in the basket or floral art classes. They are in their element when allowed to display their charms with some added accessory like those attractive baskets, bowls or displays. If I had to select just one group from all the dahlias that would please everyone, I would certainly have to go for the Waterlilies.

'Christopher Taylor'
A beautiful mid-red-flowered variety with strong growth and fine exhibition form. Relatively new, it soon attracted the attention of show folk. Rather taller than some at 1.35 m (4½ ft).

'Gerrie Hoek'
This lovely pink described above would join any list of recommended dahlias. Probably the one dahlia known by every gardener who ever planted one of these.

'Glorie van Heemstede'
A yellow *par excellence* (described above) that seems to go on forever. No garden should be without this marvellous cut flower that can equally well enhance your garden display.

'Peace Pact'
A purest white Waterlily-flowered dahlia, well suited for exhibition. This recently introduced Dutch beauty wins regularly all over the country. Plants grow around 1.05 m (3½ ft) high.

Opposite: 'Comet' (Anemone flowered) bears impressive 7.5–10 cm (3–4 in) diameter blooms.

'Porcelain'
This recently introduced award-winning Waterlily dahlia is a delicate blend of lilac and white, as befits its name. Ideal for garden decoration or cutting at 1.05 m (3½ ft).

'Twiggy'
A prolific cut flower that guarantees masses of waterlily type blooms in darkish pink with some yellow at the base. Average height around 90 cm (3 ft).

'Vicky Crutchfield'
Raised in Sussex, this is another dark pink beauty which combines two shades of that colour. Another excellent cut flower that will also exhibit well. Height 90 cm (3 ft).

Group 5. Decorative-flowered

This is the most prolific of all the ten dahlia sections, perhaps because they are so robust. There is no doubt that these varieties, which can yield dahlia blooms from 7.5 cm (3 in) in diameter to a massive 35–37.5 cm (14–15 in) in the giant-flowered types, have a built-in power that enables them to be used for any purpose – even the delicate art of flower arranging. All of this group are fully double-flowered. The outer florets are broad and generally flat (sometimes slightly twisted) but mostly reflex to the stem to give you a deep, full bloom. Naturally, such qualifications guarantee that many Decorative cultivars are the darlings of the exhibition fraternity. Indeed, many of our finest show blooms appear in this section, whether your penchant is for the smaller types or the football-sized giants. But it would be wrong to give the impression that this group is solely for the showman, because there are hundreds of varieties suitable for cut flowers or for garden decoration. The powerful root system that supports this form guarantees an almost unlimited supply of dahlias for cutting, and it is not unusual to have a bush carrying 60–80 blooms and buds at once during the season. The growth needed for that can also generate the large-flowered (20–25 cm/8–10 in in diameter) and the giants (above 25 cm/10 in across). While growth must be restricted to obtain such large dahlias (a subject dealt with in a later chapter) it is possible, contrary to popular belief, to grow the largest dahlias in the open garden rather than having to use covered areas or a greenhouse. Among the smaller Decorative-flowered types are the smalls and miniatures, mostly under 13 cm (5 in) in diameter with the miniatures often less than 8 cm (3 in). Here you will find some lovely varieties most useful for the flower arranger or the gardener intent on getting more blooms per square yard from his or her plot! The Decoratives are one of the most popular of the ten sections of dahlias and deservedly so.

GIANTS AND LARGE

'Almand's Climax'
A California-raised giant Decorative in lilac and white blends, this top winner will grow easily to 30 cm (1 ft) in diameter. Plants 1.05 m (3½ ft).

'Alvas Supreme'
Considered by most dahlia enthusiasts to be the very best giant Decorative in circulation today. A bright yellow from New Zealand, it finishes like a football by reflexing right back to the stem. Height 90 cm (3 ft).

'Amaran Relish'
A world-class giant raised in Britain, a fairly rare event. This well-formed, light bronze beauty from Cornwall took 'Best Giant in Show' on its maiden appearance at the National Show, London, 1988. 1.05 m (3½ ft).

'Blithe Spirit'
This scarlet-tipped white large Decorative from Holland is not everyone's cup of tea, but it is a personal favourite. Grow it correctly and the judges cannot help but give you a prize! Height 1.05 m (3½ ft).

'Bonaventure'
A yellow and bronze blend recently arrived from the USA. A truly big dahlia this, the largest giant we have had for many years. Easy to grow to perfection with powerful stems that hold the bloom correctly. 1.2 m (4 ft).

'Camano Titan'
This massive American dahlia is another of recent introduction. Light bronze, buff and some pink intermingle here. On occasion the form will be of Semi-cactus type. Plants 1.2 m (4 ft) high.

'Go American'
One of the longest serving giant Decoratives we have and one of the most successful. Deep bronze on 1.05 m

(3½ft) bushes, this American import is very easy to grow and would suit the beginner.

'Hamari Gold'
Coloured as its name, this is British raised, from one of the world's best dahlia hybridists, W. Ensum of Worcester Park, Surrey. Very easy to grow so excellent for the novice. Plants only 1.05m (3ft) high.

'Holland Festival'
The most colourful giant Decorative we have. Big blooms can be grown (over 30cm (1ft) wide on occasion) in bright flame-orange, tipped white. Another that definitely influences the judges when you get it right. Plants 1.2m (4ft) tall.

'Kidd's Climax'
This New Zealander is 20 years old, yet no self-respecting giant-lover would be without it. Pink and yellow, it wins everywhere and thrives in any type of soil. Low grower, around 90cm (3ft).

'Lula Pattie'
Once reputed to be the world's largest dahlia. Its white petals can get a little unkempt if grown incorrectly, but once mastered it wins prizes. Plants around 1.05m (3½ft) with stems as thick as broomhandles! Yes, you're right, it's American.

'Night Editor'
A personal favourite in the giant decorative group. Rich purple, it has a fine well-defined form and has been winning prizes at top level for over 30 years. Plants some 1.05m (3½ft) tall.

'Polyand'
The leading large decorative variety for show work. This 25-year-old pink veteran from Australia has formal petalling that wins it prizes. Easy to grow, height 1.2m (4ft).

'Silver City'
A white, raised in Leicestershire. Another with the formal petalling that wins on the show bench. Strong stems; an easy grower 1.05m (3½ft) high.

'White Alvas'
Sport of leading variety 'Alvas Supreme' (see above) coloured as name. It is as easy to grow as its parent and just as likely to win top awards. Plant height about 1.05m (3½ft).

MEDIUM & SMALL FLOWERED INCLUDING SOME MINIATURES

'Abridge Taffy'
One of our best Miniatures for show work and for cut flowers. White, there is little room for criticism of this one – it is a real cracker. Height 1.2m (4ft).

'Alltami Classic'
A Medium Decorative with blooms 20cm (8in) in diameter. Soft yellow, it has an easy growth habit and so is suitable for the beginner. Very formal on plants some 1.05m (3½ft) high.

'Angora'
This white beauty will appeal to many gardeners looking for something unusual: fimbriated (split) petal ends give it the appearance of a carnation. Grows to around 90cm (3ft) high and recommended as a cut flower.

Opposite: *The Collerette 'Chimborazo' is one of the most distinguished of its class, with scarlet blooms set off by golden collars. Understandably coveted as a cut flower and for the show bench. Above: 'Clair de Lune' – it means 'moonlight' – is a lovely soft yellow Collerette with a role of its own as a cut flower and garden variety.*

'B. J. Beauty'
This well-formed white has been dominating the Medium Decoratives for several years now. Not because it is perfect – it is not. We have a dearth of first-class Medium Decoratives and this will do for showmen until something better happens along. Height around 1.05 m (3½ ft).

'Cherry Wine'
An eye-catching red as its name indicates. Of decorative form on long, cuttable stems, it blooms persistently throughout the long season and is a guaranteed vase-filler. Grows to around 1.05 m (3½ ft).

'Chorus Girl'
A name that most dahlia lovers will know, because this Scottish raised Miniature in mid-pink is one of the most popular cut flowers ever raised. Almost 40 years old, this Decorative will give you first-class service no matter what your soil or standard of cultivation. Grows to 90 cm (3 ft).

'David Howard'
An orange Miniature with blooms around 8–10 cm (3–4 in) across. Distinctive for its dark, coppery foliage that sets off the flowers dramatically. A true eye-catcher at 75 cm (2½ ft), needing very little support.

'Edinburgh'
Another veteran from Scotland that has been around for 40 years and took an Award of Merit at Wisley Trials in 1951. It still offers a mass of lovely purple-tipped white blooms every summer. Grows to 1.05 m (3½ ft).

'Hamari Fiesta'
A small-flowered Decorative that shows that kind of dahlia at its flamboyant best. A bright golden-yellow, tipped scarlet, it literally lights up any garden. The perfect cut flower or garden display dahlia. 90 cm (3 ft) tall.

'Jescot Jim'
Not many of the old 'Jescot' cut flower dahlias are left in commerce, but this butter-yellow Small Decorative is one. 'Jescots', raised in Hertfordshire, ruled the dahlia roost in Britain at one time, and could be guaranteed to supply masses of bloom. This one grows around 90 cm (3 ft) high.

'Kung Fu'
A strange name for a flower, but this brilliant red cut flower and show dahlia – a dual-purpose variety – will give you hosts of blooms to fill vases all summer. A Small Decorative making a plant 1.05 m (3½ ft) high.

'Lady Linda'
A leading yellow Small Decorative of immaculate form. A strong grower, this top winner grows to 90 cm (3 ft) or so high. Thoroughly recommended for beginners.

'Le Batts Premier' is from the U.S.A.,
and whilst that country is best noted for the giant-flowered varieties, this Small Decorative has all the promise of a winner, whether for exhibition or cut flower. A brand new variety released during the spring of 1989. 1.05 m (3½ ft) high.

'Margaret Anne'
This pale yellow Miniature wins nationwide with consummate ease. Perhaps the best Miniature Decorative we have, which is equally able to provide a continuous supply of cut blooms. 1.05 m (3½ ft) tall.

'Master Alan'
If you are looking for a reliable, essential white for your vases, this is it. Strong stems and neatly formed Miniature Decorative blooms of purest white make this, for me, a three star variety. Height around 90 cm (3 ft).

'Meian', like many new arrivals from
Japan, is somewhat different in form and colour to many of our home-bred dahlias. A Medium Decorative, it does not have classical show form, but as a garden or cut flower dahlia the strong growth and delightful colouring will make it popular.

'Nationwide'
This variety, a blend of light bronze and yellow, was chosen by the National Dahlia Society to celebrate their Centenary in 1981. It was a great success, and this Northumberland-raised Small Decorative is still highly rated as a cut flower. Plants 1.05 m (3½ ft) high.

'Nina Chester'
The perfect variety for show work. A Small Decorative raised in Essex with a record of wins as long as your arm, it is white with an occasional lavender flush on the outer petal edges. Plants around 1.05 m (3½ ft) tall.

'Orange Robin'
Sport from famous 'Rothesay Robin' (see below), coloured as name. Masses of cuttable dahlias from first flowering to frost. 1.2 m (4 ft) high.

'Poppa Jim'
A Yorkshire introduction with a fine record. Rich deep purple, it stands on strong stems and will be a delight in your garden if you are not tempted to cut it for your vases. A Small Decorative that makes a plant around 1.05 m (3½ ft) high.

'Requiem'
Despite its name it is far from gloomy, with rich purple hues that are a foil for many of the pastel shades you might be growing. A Decorative in the Small group (blooms around 15 cm (6 in) in diameter). Height 1.05 m (3½ ft).

'Rothesay Robin'
This Scottish variety is a very pleasant mixture of bronze and dark pink. Small Decorative dimensions, with long stems suitable for cutting or exhibition, where it has established itself so well. Plants around 1.2 m (4 ft), sometimes a little taller.

'Ruskin Diane'
Competes fiercely with its rival 'Lady Linda' (see above) for top honours in the Small Decorative group. Both yellow, there is little to choose between them as they regularly top the popularity and prize-winning charts. Height in the region of 1.05 m (3½ ft).

'Scarborough Centenary'
A fine cut flower named by its Yorkshire raiser after a fine event. Small Decorative, its very formal blooms are light pink and bright yellow, a rare combination. Grows around 1.2 m (4 ft) high.

'Senzoe Ursula'
A blend of deep lilac and white of recent arrival that has risen in the charts to become one of our most favoured varieties for show work. A Small Decorative of immaculate form, it produces well from mid-summer to mid-autumn. Plants taller than average at 1.2 m (4 ft).

'Sherwood Standard'
A Nottinghamshire introduction, this is one of the top Medium Decoratives in orange blends with the formal petalling modern dahlias require to win. Plants around 90 cm (3 ft) high. A 'must' if you are showing in this section.

'Spencer'
Raised in Northamptonshire and named after Princess Diana's family, this elegant pink Small Decorative is a dual-purpose winner. Plants grow around 1.05 m (3½ ft) tall.

Group 6. Ball Dahlias

These have blooms of spherical shape, rather like a tennis ball. Some 20 or more years ago the National Dahlia Society, searching for complete international agreement on classification, agreed to the American term 'Ball' for this form of dahlia. This wasn't universally popular, as our own term, used since the type was first discovered in Victorian times, was Double Show and Fancy – Show being a variety of one colour, while Fancy was a mix or blend of two or more colours. A flamboyant title, but one that was entirely British in conception. Many of us still mourn the passing of the familiar D.S.F.s. This group has all-double blooms, that are, of necessity, ball shaped. Occasionally, they are flattened on the top of the bloom, but all the florets are blunt or rounded at the tips, with the margins spirally arranged and involute for more than half their length, producing the ball shape.

Their neat geometric appearance makes them attractive to many gardeners who grow this strong-stemmed section for cut flowers, often to the exclusion of many of the other interesting types. There are colour variations where yellows blend with purples, and those bright scarlets, so beloved by

Opposite: *'La Cierva', raised in Holland, is popular as an exhibition bloom, its aristocratic white-collared scarlet blooms winning many prizes.*
Above: *'Rosalie' is a new Collerette dahlia that is equally at home in your garden, flower arrangement or, yes, on the show bench!*

dahlia enthusiasts, have a nestling centre of butter yellow. There is no blue, of course, but you can have an array of lavenders, lilacs and mauves to come as close as we will ever get to it.

Plants vary considerably in height, so be careful when you buy in plants to look at the height in your nurseryman's catalogue. The smallest blooms are carried on bushes just 75cm (2½ft) high, but some can exceed 1.8m (6ft) in height. The latter are perfect garden dahlias for the back of a modern planting scheme. Blooms range from 8cm (3in) in diameter to a maximum of 15cm (6in) – an ideal size for the cut flower specialist. They are exceedingly popular for exhibition, and championships are staged annually for this old Victorian favourite. In fact when the last Hanoverian monarch was on the throne in Britain, dahlia shows consisted of nothing but Ball or D.S.F. dahlias. Some 24 vases could be called for in one exhibit, each vase to contain 10 blooms of one variety. Ask a showman to produce that sort of exhibit nowadays and you're likely to have a strike on your hands!

SELECTED BALL DAHLIAS
(SMALLS AND MINIATURES)

'Bonny Blue'
Many of my colleagues would look askance at my selection of this 40-year-old veteran from Scotland, but its deep lilac hues have graced gardens all over the world, and I would always want a plant or two in my garden. Makes fine tubers that keep well, maybe the secret of its longevity. Plants grow 1.05 m (3½ ft) high.

'Cherida'
A Miniature Ball dahlia that has received many awards, this strong-growing beauty is a mixture of bronze and lilac and the perfect flower arranger's variety. Grows to around 90 cm (3 ft) tall with blooms only 8–10 cm (3–4 in) in diameter.

'Connoisseur's Choice'
This Dutch Miniature Ball dahlia, bright flame in colour, has always been one of my favourite cut flowers. It started life as a show variety but is much better suited to vases indoors. Rather tall at 1.35 m (4½ ft).

'Crichton Honey'
This Miniature Ball from County Durham, coloured as its name, has developed an international reputation. A frenetic producer of blooms with height around 1.05 m (3½ ft).

'L'Ancresse'
A classic white with form to match, this Miniature Ball from Surrey (not the Channel Islands, as you might think) is well suited for exhibition or cut flowers. Plant height 1.05 m (3½ ft).

'Risca Miner'
A full-sized Ball dahlia (blooms around 15 cm (6 in) in diameter), this is the richest deep purple imaginable. With long stems on robust plants around 1.2 m (4 ft) high, this will cut for you or win those red cards.

'Rothesay Superb'
A Scottish-raised scarlet Miniature Ball. Good for showing and cutting on plants some 1.05 m (3½ ft) high.

'Wootton Cupid'
A Miniature blend of pinks that produces show and cut flower blooms with equal ease. Height 1.05 m (3½ ft).

Group 7. Pompon Dahlias

A Miniature form of the Ball dahlia, described above. Officially, Pompons should not exceed 52 mm (2 in) in diameter. Any that do so consistently would be moved to the Ball group by the classification committee. Some international dahlia organizations, notably the Dutch and other Continentals, persistently ignore this and include in their Pompon grouping dahlias of Ball and even Decorative form up to 8 cm (3 in) or more in diameter. If you are intending to exhibit Pompon dahlias in this country, beware of the foreign size limits. Arrange some Dutch pretenders in a vase and you will run foul of the disqualification rules framed by our own National Dahlia Society, which say that pompons must not exceed 52 mm (2 in) across. To ensure the ruling is correct, they supply their judges with rings that must pass cleanly over the Pompon in question without touching the petals.

A smaller version of the Ball form, the Pompon first came to light in Germany around 1900. French nurserymen were so taken with these exquisite little babies that they imported early stock, then added the name 'pompon' which, it is said, came from the 'bobble' on French sailors' caps. The best Pompons come from Australia, where the seeds set far more easily for their hybridists in the sunny climate, than our own raisers find, especially in a wet autumn, when it can be difficult to obtain suitable seeds. Yet it is internationally agreed that here in Britain we have the finest growers of Pompons in the world.

Several of them have produced their own seedlings in recent years, many as good as those that arrive here from Australia. With such a wealth of top Pompon growers, competition in this country is first class. Many might believe that growing and showing these little beauties would be easy, but I have to disillusion you. Poms grow readily enough, but there are so many faults and pitfalls to overcome with them that only the best exhibitors survive as top showmen.

They are wonderful for garden use and as cut flowers, offering a continuous supply of minute blooms on wiry stems throughout the season. They have no equal for arranging in vases, staying put wherever they are placed to the delight of the flower arranger or floral artist. Ask any member of a floral art society what form of dahlia is their favourite and four out of five will plump for the Pompon!

'Diana Gregory'
One of the oldest Poms we have, a lilac from Australia. It is still well grown by top exhibitors and makes a fine garden plant. 90 cm (3 ft) tall.

'Hallmark'
Frequently given 'Best in Show' nowadays and qualifies as the favourite of several of Britain's top showfolk. With blooms a mixture of lilac and dark pink, it has no faults. Grows to around 90 cm (3 ft).

'Little Sally'
A Pom you will love! Bright flame-red, each plant covers itself with bloom throughout the summer. Not a low grower as so many expect of Poms, plants getting up to 90 cm (3 ft) or so high.

'Moor Place'
The perfect dual-purpose Pom. Excellent for show but equally at home with the cut flower enthusiast or the flower arranger. A rich royal purple, its stems are adequate for all needs and the plants a little higher than normal at 1.05 m (3½ ft).

'Pensford Marion'
A dark pink raised by National Champion Frank Newbery of Bristol, of show-winning form as you might expect. It also serves well as a prolific cut flower. 90 cm (3 ft) tall.

'Small World'
The best white Pompon we have. It is stocked by all the top growers which is recommendation enough. Ideal for show, making bushes some 90 cm (3 ft) high.

'Tutankhamun'
Very popular white pompon suitable for cut flowers or floral art. Easy to grow on fairly low bushes around 75 cm (2½ ft) high.

'Willo Flecks'
The famous 'Willo' prefix is from Australian raiser Norman Williams, considered the best ever raiser of this

Opposite: *Waterlily variety 'Glorie van Heemstede' is a fine yellow that has really stayed the pace, having been a winner since 1947.*
Below: *Dutch introduction 'Peace Pact' is a purest white Waterlily variety that wins many prizes at shows, besides making a good 1.05 m (3½ ft) border plant.*

type of dahlia. 'Flecks' is a yellow and red variety good for all purposes. 90 cm (3 ft) tall.

'Willo's Violet'
Perhaps the best of all Mr Williams' many varieties. Four decades old, yet still wins and offers cut blooms in abundance. 90 cm (3 ft) high.

Group 8. Cactus-flowered

Most gardeners know these simply as 'the spiky ones'. The name came from the similarity of the mature bloom to that of the tropical cactus flower, but there the similarity ends. This group has

so many things going for it that it must rank among the most popular of all types of dahlia. Originally discovered in Holland from a batch of tubers and seeds sent to a Utrecht grower in the 1880s, this form appeared right out of the blue. The excited Dutchman was quick to name the newcomer *D. juarezii* after a Mexican President and very soon every enthusiast in Europe was seeking stock of this long-petalled beauty with rolled and pointed florets. It was introduced into commerce by the early 1890s and has never looked back, being a firm favourite all over the world.

The reasons for this are quickly apparent if you grow Cactus-flowered varieties. They are firm of stem with the bloom's head held correctly and offer every colour – except for that blue! They are easy to grow to perfection, and I would always recommend Cactus dahlias to a beginner who, in his or her first dahlia season could well find he or she had achieved perfection first time round.

Like the Decoratives, Cactus-flowered dahlias can produce blooms only 8 cm (3 in) across, but can also give dahlias exceeding the magical 30 cm (12 in) diameter. Hence they are highly popular for exhibition and you will see more Cactus varieties (and their close relatives the Semi-cactus types, which I will come to in a moment) on the showbench than any other form. It is possibly the way in which the florets of a well-grown Cactus dahlia fan out that makes it so attractive. Certainly a massed entry in a full range of colours staged at one of our national shows is an awe-inspiring sight, even to a veteran like me.

The green baize cloth of the exhibition hall is not the only key place for the Cactus dahlia, because within their colourful ranks there is a host of cut flower and garden varieties to delight everyone, even the most fastidious. The tiny Miniatures, like stars, only 8 cm (3 in) across vie with the larger Small-flowered and Medium varieties to fill vases nationwide all summer. If ever one group deserved the title given to dahlias in general – the 'cut and come again flower' – the Cactus get that honour from me. They grow to various heights, with the tallest at 1.8 m (6 ft) or more, while some bloom profusely on bushes a mere 75 cm (2½ ft) high. Light disbudding produces a forest of blooms from which you can take armfuls of flowers daily, yet not see where they have been. Again, every colour except blue is yours for the asking. They include lovely bicolours, blends of several colours, and variegated blooms that are a mosaic of several primary colours. This type of dahlia embraces everything that is good about this flower – you should try some for yourself.

'Athalie'
A mixture of dark pink and bronze, this Small Cactus appears regularly in the show winners' analysis published by the National Dahlia Society. Exquisitely formed blooms on plants some 1.05 m (3½ ft) high.

'Banker'
A rare Medium Cactus, the pure rolled-petal Cactus form. A bright red, this

Dutch introduction has been used for years with great success. Plants some 1.2 m (4 ft) high.

'Cryfield Max'
One of the best of the yellow Small Cactus, good for show and for bloom production. The form is perfect, and while not the easiest of dahlias to get to perfection, it has a record of success that makes it essential in any collection. Height 1.05 m (3½ ft).

'Dana Audrey'
A fairly new arrival, a mix of purple and red – quite unusual. This is a Miniature Cactus, also rare, with blooms only 8–10 cm (3–4 in) across. Plants 90 cm (3 ft) high.

'Dana Iris'
A brilliant red Small Cactus. The spiky beauty of this long-stemmed cut flower is quite striking. Given an Award (Highly Commended) at Wisley. Height 1.05 m (3½ ft).

'Doris Day'
I had to include dear old 'Doris Day' in my selection – a marvellous cut flower about to celebrate her 40th birthday. Dutch raised, despite the name, a scarlet Small Cactus growing 90 cm (3 ft) or so high.

'Klankstad Kerkrade'
Now 34 years old and still winning prizes, this is the supreme all-time winner for me and one that dahlia lovers of the last two generations regard with most affection. An easily grown sulphur yellow Small Cactus, it makes a prolific plant 1.2 m (4 ft) or so tall.

'Majestic Athalie'
A pink (with some yellow) sport of 'Athalie', this is a showman's favourite yet fine for a beginner. A Small Cactus like its parent, it will also yield masses of cut blooms for your vases. 1.05 m (3½ ft) high.

'Miyako Bijin'
'Miyako Bijin' is another from the Land of the Rising Sun that brings a splash of unusual colour to your garden. A Cactus in the medium size range, this bright beauty flowers in mid-summer and continues offering well-formed blooms until the first frosts of winter, usually in late October. 90 cm (3 ft) high.

'Park Princess'
As its name implies, this is a variety you can use for bedding as well as cutting. A Dutch import, this pink dual-purpose dahlia grows only 60 cm (2 ft) high and needs minimal staking. Flower size 8–10 cm (3–4 in) diameter. For maximum effect, plant fairly closely, say around 23 cm (9 in) apart.

'Rokesley Mini'
Arguably the best Miniature Cactus we have today. A white that develops perfectly formed show blooms around 10 cm (4 in) in diameter and is also useful as a cut flower. Despite the Miniature tag, plants are still around 1.05 m (3½ ft) high.

'Shy Princess'
Probably the best *pure* Cactus we have. A white of first-class exhibition form, it is a strong grower. Plants tend to be rather tall, sometimes topping 1.8 m (6 ft). One for the back of a border? Flower size 15–20 cm (6–8 in) diameter.

Above: 'Porcelain', a Waterlily variety, is a lovely delicate lilac and white, valued alike for garden display and as a cut flower.

Opposite: 'Twiggy', also a Waterlily variety, is a prolific producer of stunning blooms, both for cutting and for effect in a display border.

Group 9. Semi-cactus-flowered

As the name suggests, they are half-way between the Cactus-flowered types on the one hand and the broader petalled Decoratives on the other. They could equally well be named Semi-decoratives, because in many instances the Decorative form predominates. Again, all cultivars are double, but while the florets are pointed, as in the Cactus-flowered, most of the petals are narrower than a Decorative's, yet broader than the tightly rolled petals of the true Cactus. The petals can be straight or incurving but must be revolute for a half or less of their length, the main difference.

We have the very largest of all dahlias among the Semi-cactus varieties – the Giant-flowered types. There are reports that some American-raised varieties can reach a massive 45cm (18in) in diameter. I have seen some of these imports grown to 38–40cm (15–16in) across the face of the bloom, but the natural result of such size is a bearding or drooping of the lower florets that in British competitions is considered a fault to be avoided. Hence our showmen aim to grow a Giant-flowered Semi-cactus bloom to approximately 30cm (12in) in diameter, to attain perfection of form as well as the recognized maximum width. Such a combination of size and form makes for greater excellence of cultivation in the eyes of our rule makers, the National Dahlia Society.

The Semi-cactus group also contains some of the most popular show varieties in the whole dahlia range, like the Small-flowered varieties and, perhaps most popular of all, the Medium-flowered Semi-cactus types. More of the latter have been raised over the years than any of the other sections, so you will find the lists bulging with an enviable selection. Strong growers, the Semi-cactus varieties have powerful stems and an unequalled growth habit. As with the Decoratives such root power is essential if you are to produce massive blooms on the Giants or long-stemmed beauties from those popular Mediums.

The colour range is on a par with the other types, again without the blue, though there is a wider list of near-blues classified as lilacs or lavenders, with the occasional mauve. Cut flower specialists could not be without some of the Semi-cactus varieties, noted for stem strength, but the flower arranger would seem to prefer the more delicate forms to the heavy robustness of this group. That is not to say that the floral artist should ignore the Semi-cactus. On the contrary, the Miniature (under 8cm (3in)) orange beauty 'Andrie's Orange' has for long been a favourite of these talented ladies. Apparently, being able to stage a tight bud, an opening bud and a fully open flower from one plant adds to its attraction. It was the sheer power of the Semi-cactus Giants that helped attract me to this group many years ago. Some of their buds can be larger than a man's closed fist, and when this spectacular act of nature unfolds into a mature flower – well, you have to grow one to experience the thrill of it!

'Andrie's Orange'
Well over 50 years old, it came here from Belgium in 1936. That it is still as popular now as then is commendation enough. A prolific, bright orange Miniature. Height 90 cm (3 ft).

'Cheerio'
Another regular favourite. A real cut flower stalwart, it came from Australia where it was raised some 30 years ago. A Small-flowered Semi-cactus, it is coloured cherry-red, tipped silver – most unusual. Height 90 cm (3 ft) high.

'Cryfield Bryn'
Sister seedling to 'Cryfield Max' (see under Cactus) this Small Semi-cactus is top of the league with showmen. Yellow, but darker than 'Max', it wins readily anywhere in the country. Plenty of cut flowers too on plants around 1.05 m (3½ ft) high.

'DeSarasate',
a little larger than some, this well-awarded Dutch Large Semi-cactus offers plenty of bloom notwithstanding its acknowledged size potential. Lightly disbudded there will be plenty of bloom to cut for your vases. A little disbudding and you have a show winner. 1.2 m (4 ft) high.

'Daleko Jupiter'
A massive Giant Semi-cactus raised in Britain (despite name). A stunning scarlet and yellow, it has been a winner on our show benches for many years and has given several sports ('Pink Jupiter' and 'Rose Jupiter', coloured as named) that are equally good. They dominate the Giant Semi-cactus section. 1.2 m (4 ft) high.

'Eastwood Moonlight'
Our leading Medium Semi-cactus, an elegant yellow, whose form, stem and growth habit leave nothing to be desired. This must be on your list if you decide to exhibit. Plants 1.35 m (4½ ft) high.

'Evening Mail'
This soft yellow Giant Semi-cactus has first class form and is easy to grow. A full deep bloom that can be 30 cm (1 ft) or more in diameter when grown to its full potential. Not for the beginner, however. Plants 1.35 m (4½ ft) tall.

'Grenidor Pastelle'
Latest sensation to hit the dahlia world, this Essex-raised lovely is a Medium Semi-cactus of stunning form in soft pink and yellow. It won nationwide on its maiden appearances in 1988, so you should note it as a dahlia with a future. Height around 1.05–1.2 m (3½–4 ft).

'Hamari Accord'
A well-formed yellow, again of recent introduction. A nice easy grower with powerful stems, it fits into the Large group with blooms around 23–25 cm (9–10 in) in diameter. Grows 1.2 m (4 ft) high and bears the 'Hamari' hallmark of the world's best dahlia hybridist – W. Ensum of Surrey. No further recommendation is needed.

'Hamari Bride'
Another with the Ensum label, but this time a Medium Semi-cactus of brilliant white. Better suited to the beginner this one, and a show variety with a first class record. Height around 1.05 m (3½ ft).

Opposite: *Sussex-raised 'Vicky Crutchfield', a Waterlily variety, is valued as an exhibition variety as well as a cut flower.*
Above: *'Amaran Relish' is a rare bird, a British raised (Cornwall) Giant Decorative. In its maiden year (1988) it won best Giant in the National Dahlia Show at the RHS Halls, London.*

'Inca Dambuster'

Another soft yellow variety. It is probably the biggest dahlia ever raised in Britain. A tall grower that needs a little experience to get to its very best. Occasionally plants will reach 1.8 m (6 ft) or more in height.

'Kiwi Brother'

Not from New Zealand, despite its name, but raised in Warwickshire. A lovely mix of pink and bronze, this is a fine show dahlia with every asset a winner needs. It will also yield a host of cut flowers on plants some 90 cm (3 ft) high. Flower size 10–15 cm (4–6 in) diameter.

'Laurence Fisher'

A bright yellow from East Anglia that swept all before it in its year of introduction in the early eighties. A Medium Semi-cactus, it will show successfully but is also adept at producing quality dahlias for your enjoyment in the garden. Height 1.35 m (4½ ft).

'Le Vonne Splinter'

A mixture of bronze shades that falls into the Giant Semi-cactus grouping. A big dahlia from the USA, where it occasionally tops the show polls. A late bloomer some 1.2 m (4 ft) tall.

'Mark Damp'

One of my own raising, named after my eldest grandson. Its peach and orange blends are most acceptable and its form what is needed for show success. Very early to flower, so would fit into the late summer show dates. A Large-flowered Semi-cactus making a plant around 1.2 m (4 ft) tall.

'Match'

Originally from South Africa, this is a startling royal purple and white bicolor. Very effective for the flower arranger and well used by the floral art ladies. Makes plants around 90 cm (3 ft) high, but not a free flowerer. Flower size 8–10 cm (3–4 in) diameter.

'Primrose Bryn'

A pale lemon sport of famous 'Cryfield Bryn' (see above). As with many acknowledged sports, it has all its parent's qualities. A first-class Small Semi-cactus for show or cut flowers. A very easy one to grow, making plants 1.05 m (3½ ft) high.

'Reginald Keene'

One of the most famous dahlias ever raised, this Large Semi-cactus is a blend of orange and flame. With its equally well-known sports, 'Salmon Keene' and 'Candy Keene', coloured as named, it regularly decimates the opposition in this class. Another you cannot be without if you aspire to winning a silver trophy. Plants 1.2 m (4 ft) high.

'So Dainty'

One of those rare Miniatures – a Semi-cactus that shows and cuts well. Its colour is a blend of light bronze and buff, difficult to describe as it varies with the type of soil. A low grower this one at 75 cm (2½ ft).

'Symbol'

This beauty is still winning prizes 40 years on, having spawned sports along the way – 'Pink Symbol', 'Salmon Symbol' and 'Rose Symbol', coloured as named – from the original orange/bronze hues. All are show aristocrats, so leave them out of your calculations at your peril! All are Medium-flowered Semi-cactus averaging 1.2 m (4 ft) high.

'Turbo'

is a brand new novelty from Holland, falling into the Medium Cactus group, perhaps the most populous group of all. The delicate orange hues ensure its popularity with cut flower enthusiasts and it certainly looks ready to make its mark on the exhibition bench.

'White Moonlight'

A sport of top winner, yellow 'Eastwood Moonlight' (see above). Has all its parent's attributes and will win for you or stand in splendour in your garden, the envy of your neighbours. Height 1.35 m (4½ ft). Flower size 15–20 cm (6–8 in) diameter.

'**Wootton Impact**' falls into the Medium Semi-cactus section, and this well-formed, long stemmed beauty is ideal for exhibition whilst making a fine plant to enhance your garden. British raised in Warwickshire. Colour is apricot/light buff. 1.35 m (4½ ft) high.

Group 10. Miscellaneous

A pigeon-hole created by the National Dahlia Society in which they can place any form or type that varies from the other nine groups. Believe me, a great many forms qualify for inclusion under this heading. The Single and Double-flowered **Orchid dahlias**, for example, have no group of their own, so they become Miscellaneous. Named after the exotic flower they resemble in form, they are not so rare as one might believe, being in great demand for flower arrangements, with famous varieties like the bronze and yellow blended 'Giraffe' and its soft pink sport, 'Pink Giraffe'. Raised in Holland some 40 years ago, they have never lost their popularity.

A form that once formed a group of its own is the free-flowering **Paeony-flowered dahlia**. Its semi-double blooms with broad petals, named after their resemblance to the paeony, have long ceased to be gardeners' favourites, but they still persist. After all, you cannot eliminate a type simply by cancelling its section and transferring it to Miscellaneous! It is in this pigeon-hole that the tiny Topmix or Lilliput varieties are found. Their 2.5 cm (1 in) wide, open-centred blooms on low bushes make them highly suitable for bedding or for planting on a patio or balcony in prepared containers. These little beauties are also indispensable for miniature arrangements in the floral art section of any show. Their colour range is so wide that you can choose where you will, apart from that missing blue.

If you are a real dahlia collector, the Miscellaneous section holds many rare delights for you. The 'look-alike' **Chrysanthemum-flowered** dahlias are really stunning. The few we have in commerce are so much like incurved chrysanthemums that I often wonder why they are not more popular. After all, they are easy to grow and give many more blooms per plant in a season than the real thing. Raised by the Dutch, they disappeared when demand from growers waned, but in recent years they have reappeared from Japan, where a number currently feature on their lists, including my favourite, scarlet and yellow 'Akita'.

And the **Carnation-flowered** dahlia? This group resembles our favourite wedding flower – basically of Decorative form, but with every petal naturally split, or, correctly, fimbriated. This splitting gives the Carnation dahlia its look-alike quality and while its colour range is somewhat restricted, the fimbriated dahlia has always enjoyed a large measure of popularity – especially on the Continent, where nurserymen who specialize in dahlias are always ready to offer their customers a wider range of forms than seem to be available from our own commercial growers.

It is something of a miracle that a

small, insignificant flower that came to us from the other side of the world almost 200 years ago with single, open-centred blooms on drooping stems should have changed so much. It is as if a completely new species has been created, mainly by European growers, justifying my suggestion that we should call them *D. Europa*!

'Akita'
A dahlia from Japan masquerading as a chrysanthemum. Deep red with some gold, the mature bloom incurves gracefully just like our classic autumn flower. Not a show bloom or a cut flower, but fascinating to have in your garden. 1.05 m (3½ ft) tall.

Above: 'Camano Titan', a well-named American Giant Decorative introduction, really will grow big – often to 35 cm (14 in) in diameter. Strictly a show bloom!
Opposite: 'Hamari Gold' is one of the most popular Giant Decoratives in commerce at the moment. A rare British-raised variety, it is easy to grow.

'Bambino'
A Lilliput or Baby dahlia, occasionally classified as a Single but more often as Miscellaneous. Its blooms are only 2.5 cm (1 in) or so in diameter, so ideal for patios, bedding or balcony decoration – perhaps even for those delicate Miniature arrangements? This one is yellow and white on plants just 30 cm (1 ft) high.

'Bishop of Llandaff'

Some 60 years old and decidedly Miscellaneous! Single blooms with ruffled, open dark red petals, but its glowing bronze foliage is the main attraction. It is still listed by a number of nurseries but I cannot say that it has ever appealed to me. Perfect, though, if you are collecting vintage dahlias.

'Exotic Dwarf'

Not a name I would have chosen for this lovely Lilliput variety. Dark pink, with blooms only 2.5 cm (1 in) or so across on plants just 30 cm (1 ft) high. Its mass of blooms in summer is a sight to behold.

'Giraffe'

It is 40 years since Dutchman Hoek from the Hague raised this little beauty. Orchid-flowered (qualifying as Miscellaneous) it is bronze and yellow and has a lovely pink sport to match. Floral art societies know it well as it blends perfectly in some of their elegant arrangements. Height around 90 cm.

'Jescot Julie'

Intriguing with its Double Orchid-flowered form and splendid dark pink and bronzy orange colouring. Another for the flower arranger. Note too its sport 'Pink Julie' with lighter shades on the reverse of the petals. Plants of both varieties 90 cm (3 ft) high.

'Kuroi Hitomi'

Described as the dahlia twin for the rose. From Japan, of course, the pink buds form into a complete replica of an opening rose-bud. It is another for interest or the collector, as it really isn't a show or cut flower. Plants vary in height, but average around 90 cm (3 ft).

'Tiny Tot'

As its name indicates, this is about the smallest dahlia we have. Photographers love to shoot this 2.5 cm (1 in) wide light pink Lilliput variety against one of the massive giants! Again, one for the floral artist or to feature on the patio. Plants just 30 cm high that need no staking.

'Tohsuikyoh'

A rather elegant Orchid-flowered dahlia, slotted into Miscellaneous, from the Land of the Rising Sun. Grows around 1.05 m (3½ ft) high. Its unusual petal formation is a blend of pastel pink and rich, creamy white. Ideal for a special arrangement.

SIZE AND ITS PART IN THE TEN GROUPS

As you will have gathered, there is a great variation in size among the ten groups I have detailed. Not all types differ like this, but the Decoratives, Cactus and Semi-cactus dahlias vary in size from Miniatures to Giants. The Ball and Waterlily-flowered varieties are limited to Miniature and Small sizes (with one Medium-flowered exception in the Waterlily group). The Pompons, as we have seen, are limited to blooms 52 mm (2 in) across. For the rest, size is considered of only relative importance and no official minimum or maximum bloom sizes have been documented. Most, however, like those contained in the Single-flowered, Anemone-flowered and Collerette forms generally grow around 10–15 cm (4–6 in) in diameter, making them ideal for the ordinary gardener who wants dahlias only for cut flowers or garden decoration.

OFFICIAL DAHLIA SIZES:

Group A	*Giant-flowered*: Usually over 254 mm (10 in) in diameter.
Group B	*Large-flowered*: Usually between 203 and 254 mm (8–10 in) in diameter.
Group C	*Medium-flowered*: Usually between 152 and 203 mm (6–8 in) in diameter.
Group D	*Small-flowered*: Usually between 102 and 152 mm (4–6 in) in diameter.
Group E	*Miniature-flowered*: Not usually more than 102 mm (4 in) in diameter.

The 'A' to 'E' sizes are used for classifying the dahlias in their bi-annual lists, but for exhibition purposes these sizes are slightly increased before any blooms are disqualified by the Society's officials for being oversize. The exhibition limits are:

Giant-flowered: No limits – to be grown as large as possible.
Large-flowered: Top limit is 260 mm (10¼ in).
Medium-flowered: Top limit is 220 mm (8¾ in).
Small-flowered: Top limit is 170 mm (6¾ in).
Miniature-flowered: Top limit is 115 mm (4½ in).
Pompon: Top limit is: 52 mm (2 in).

As this table shows, various margins are offered for exhibition, ranging from only 6 mm (¼ in) on the Large types to 13 mm (½ in) on the Miniatures, with no extra allowance for the Pompon growers.

Showmen are given quite a generous amount of room to manoeuvre in some sections, with the 18 mm (¾ in) allowance. Being allowed to grow this far over the correct classification sizes would seem a satisfactory solution to what has always been a contentious matter among dahlia enthusiasts. The most difficult aspect is that showmen sometimes stage blooms for exhibition a few hours before they are actually judged. During this interval dahlia blooms tend to expand a little, especially the Pompons. This makes it possible to leave an exhibit at midnight, having 'ringed' all the dahlia blooms to ensure that they are not oversize, and then find on returning after judging that the dreaded 'N.A.S.' (Not according to schedule) has been marked on the entry card. So it would seem wise to choose varieties that naturally grow below the specified limits. But ambitious exhibitors will always opt for those that sail very close to the disqualification limits, which seems to me to be the real cause for discontent. Perhaps some future conference of Britain's dahlia enthusiasts will settle this argument.

COLOUR IN DAHLIAS

The dahlia's chief asset, colour, has just as important a part to play as form and size, and this is dealt with in the Appendix (see p. 118).

CHAPTER FOUR

GENERAL CULTIVATION

Dahlias are among the most obliging of our summer ornamentals when it comes to cultivation. They will bloom in almost any soil or situation. To get the best from your dahlias takes a little understanding and care.

For most dahlia lovers this all starts in the autumn, when frost has blackened their foliage and the season is at an end. The life of your stock plants now hangs in the balance, because the roots that will perpetuate them are vulnerable to winter weather. So lifting and storing them is urgent. The new season, then, arises from the ashes of the previous one in the shape of those gnarled, awkward-looking tubers.

Their appearance can be misleading too. Giant fattened roots weighing 6.5 kg (14 lb) or more could have developed from a plant that has yielded only a meagre crop of tiny blooms, while a stringy thin tuber could have sustained giant blooms 30 cm (1 ft) across. There is, in fact, little correlation between plant and root, a mystery this Mexican immigrant keeps to itself.

When the roots have been successfully stored for the winter, ready to be used for propagation the next spring (see next chapter), the plot in which they have been growing needs to be revitalized. All good gardeners agree that you cannot take from the soil anything that you do not put into it, so if you want to maintain a supply of top quality blooms, this is the time to act.

A SUITABLE SITE

I would first suggest that you review the site chosen for growing your dahlias. Avoid one where nearby tall trees, high shrubs or walls cast shade. Far better to select a sunny open central position, away from such obstacles that only draw the plants so that they develop thin weak stems unable to hold the blooms properly erect. Distant trees, however, could shield them from the fierce heat of the midsummer sun. Not everyone has the scope to choose where in their garden a certain flower will grow, but even if you have to move other plants to make a good-sized dahlia plot, you will find it of lasting benefit.

One particular dislike they have is of herbaceous borders. What a temptation it is to plant your dahlias in this jungle of roots and stems! You will have seen it done in many famous gardens here and abroad, but dahlias hate having to fight for root room with other summer flowers. When it becomes a running battle with lupins, delphiniums and other thong-rooted perennials, they are likely to perform poorly or give up altogether. To help you understand this, I should explain that the sub-tropical dahlia's root system is massive, yet fragile. A web of fine feeding roots spreads out some 90 cm (3 ft) in all directions from the carrot-like tubers, which take a whole season to form. Given the opportunity to forage in a plot to themselves, they will help produce the miracles of form, colour, height and shape that we expect from our dahlias – but not otherwise.

DRAINAGE

Another aspect of that derelict autumn plot you must consider seriously is drainage. If it is poorly drained, you must do something about it, for dahlias detest having to grow in soggy soil. To improve their growing conditions, raise the plot slightly. My own soil used to be like that until I raised my whole dahlia plot some 20–25 cm (8–10 in) by simply boarding the edge. Set a 20 cm (8 in) board or two courses of bricks or suitable stones in place, then you can throw the soil forward as you dig. Keep doing this as you work across the plot and you will end up with an extra 20–25 cm (8–10 in) depth of soil. Being good top soil, it will drain freely right away. The dahlias' fine roots need only that sort of depth to perform splendidly. If you find you need a little more to provide really efficient drainage, then just raise the boards or bricks a little higher.

DIGGING

Some gardeners will tell you that the soil is better left undisturbed for the winter, and if it is very light soil, not turned or prepared for planting until the spring. But my own soil in the Midlands is rather heavier than that of my fellow enthusiasts in the South, most of whom would agree that it is essential to expose the soil on the dahlia plot before hard winter frosts arrive. By roughly digging over the plot you can expose it to the full action of the frost. Alternate freezing and thawing will break down the clods to a nice workable condition by the time you need to prepare it to take the young plants or seedlings next spring.

FEEDING

While you are directing so much energy into turning your soil and exposing it to winter's helping hand, why not improve its food value by adding something to it? This will depend largely on what you can obtain. I know it is not so easy to come by stable or farmyard manure or even mushroom compost, but if you can get them, barrow them all in, provided they have been well matured, and use a barrow-load to each square metre. Mix it in by simply folding it into the trench you make while digging. If you are tackling a drainage problem at the same time, your trench will be even better.

1. *To give dahlias a good start, work compost or well-rotted manure into the soil, where the dahlias are to be set.*

Above: *'Le Batts Premier', a well-formed Small Decorative on strong stems. This variety can equally well be grown for cutting and for exhibition.*

Opposite: *'Meian' is one of many Japanese varieties that are appearing on the European market. This one is a startling bicolour in the Medium Decorative class. On release in 1990.*

If you cannot obtain any manure or spent mushroom compost, use garden compost (Fig. 1). Everyone can build a compost heap. My twin heaps – one accumulating, the other being gradually used – are active the whole year. Every scrap of organic waste is spread on the heap – grass and shrub clippings, old turf, brassica stalks and annual plants from the flower beds. My wife makes her daily contribution of kitchen waste, vacuum cleaner dust, cotton and wool waste – anything that will rot down.

To every 15 cm (6 in) layer I add some activator – either a high-nitrogen fertilizer like Phostrogen, or one of the advertized brands of compost maker. This is then sandwiched by a similar depth of garden soil which blends with the organic material to make good compost. From late autumn until the return of the warmer weather, I keep the heaps covered, first by thatching them with the masses of foliage I get from the dahlias, then later with heavy-gauge polythene sheeting, weighted down with large stones.

It takes four to six months for my compost heaps to mature, after which the material is added to the dahlia plot at the most convenient time. If a batch is ready by early spring, I barrow the whole heap on to the dahlia beds, spread it evenly, then fork it in. Later in the year the compost is used as a mulch, a subject I will deal with later in this chapter. I must stress how vital it is to improve the soil while you are preparing it for the next season. Anything you add must be bulky and organic. It is little use adding bone meal or hoof and horn, for example, in the autumn. By spring they will have been leached away by winter rains or devoured by worms. Far better to hold back such luxuries until the time is right to add them, in mid to late spring.

PLANTING OUT

By virtue of their very nature, you cannot plant dahlias out in the open garden until late spring, when all fear of frost is past (Fig. 2). In the North and Scotland you might even need to wait until early summer before risking your plants' tender leaves outdoors. This may seem a disadvantage when other flowers like sweet peas and chrysanthemums are already out and thriving, but it does give you a magnificent opportunity to prepare the soil thoroughly for your young dahlias.

As we shall see in the next chapter, young dahlias may be seedlings, freshly rooted cuttings or, most popular of all, old tubers or parts of them. All, but for the old tubers, must wait until frosts are over. This will free mid to late spring for preparing the ground. If your winter cultivation has been successful – and it is surprising how much help you get from nature when you co-operate with her – the soil will break down easily. Top dress the entire area with 115–170 gm/m² (4–6 oz per sq yd) of bone meal and lightly fork it in, or if the weather is co-operative leave the spring rains to wash it in. Your dahlia bed is now ready for the long season of care that lasts till autumn. But you have one more decision to make before planting can begin.

2. Planting: position the plant close to a support cane in a hole slightly larger than the root ball. Firm the plant in well, leaving a small depression to facilitate watering later on.

□ EASY CARE BEDS

If you have set aside a special plot for your dahlias, you can go one step further and make it an efficient working area. Many dahlia growers now divide their plots into long narrow beds, each about 1.2 m (4 ft) wide and as long as the area will allow. Each bed can take a double row of dahlias with a service path 60 cm (2 ft) wide between them (Fig. 3). Some dahlia lovers pave these paths permanently with slabs or concrete, but I prefer grass paths myself. These can be neatly mown during the

summer and occasionally lifted and cultivated so you can alter their direction and no part of the plot becomes exhausted.

The value of these service paths becomes obvious as the dahlias grow. The plants are as slim as a pencil in late spring, but by late summer you can have bushes with a girth of 3–3.7 m (10–12 ft) with the bases of the stems as thick as a man's wrist. It would be difficult to move among such giants without damaging them unless the beds contained only a double row of plants. It is then easy to lean across from the paths to water, tie in, disbud, feed and later cut the dahlia blooms.

□ PLANTING TECHNIQUE

Having prepared the beds properly, it remains for you to set out the dahlias carefully. While dahlia plants will have to wait until after the frosts, the tubers, usually taken from store in mid to late spring, will have made no new shoots, so they can be planted out about 13 cm (5 in) deep and covered with peat or soil. First mark out the plot with canes spaced about 60 cm (2 ft) apart, then dig a hole at each position to take whatever size tuber you have. If you do this in mid to late spring, new frost-tender growth will not break surface until spring is almost over when any danger is probably past. If shoots do appear when frost is forecast, cover them by drawing soil up and over them, as you would potatoes, or protect each plant with a large pot or box. Only cover them at night, of course, removing the soil, pots or boxes each morning.

3. Ideally, plant dahlias in a plot or bed of their own, with service paths running between so that routine tasks like watering, spraying and cutting can be performed in comfort and without risking damage to the plants.

Mark out your dahlia beds in the same way for the rest of your plantings. A 60 cm (2 ft) spacing is only a rough guide, but most gardeners allow this to make way for their massive development later. The canes can look quite odd when put in at planting time, but their value soon becomes apparent as the foliage burgeons dramatically. By late summer, when the first flowers start to open, they are hidden from sight.

When setting out the plants, seedlings or tuber divisions, encourage them to make early root development. Put a spadeful of well rotted compost, manure or soilless compost into each planting hole, as close to the marker cane as possible. Such boosters will give your dahlias' roots a good start. Be sure to tie tall plants carefully to their marker canes to avoid any wind damage. Once the plants are set out, hoe the entire plot regularly to keep down weeds and aerate the soil around the plants to encourage root development, which starts within days of planting.

'STOPPING'

By quite early in summer the young plants will have taken a firm hold and it is time to start turning them into productive dahlias. This involves removing the main growing point, oddly referred to as 'stopping' the plant, when it actually helps the dahlia develop into a

fine bush. The many shoots in the leaf axils on the main stem benefit from the stopping by growing upwards and outwards, each destined to carry the first blooms of summer.

'Ruskin Diane', raised on Merseyside, is one of our leading exhibition Small Decoratives. Beautiful form and growth habit make this so.

SUPPORT

As this growth continues the plants will need extra support, so add more canes. By setting two canes in front of each plant, you will create a triangle around it and it will be simple to wind string or fillis around this 'cage' to hold the plants firmly, yet without any strain on its stems or, later, its blooms (Fig. 4).

Some professional growers use other methods of support. At the Royal Hor-ticultural Society's Wisley Garden they provide a horizontally arranged tightly stretched 15cm (6in) square mesh of wire. The young plants beneath it soon find that they can thrust through this barrier and in so doing support themselves. This certainly saves the chore of tying in, as you have to with the three-cane system I use, but you would have to tolerate some damage as the plants sway in the wind and are pushed against the wire, which occasionally cuts or severs them. As the blooms at Wisley are not cut for vases in the home or on

4. *By tying in the growing plants regularly, you will ensure that they do not keel over in high winds.*

5. *After planting, keep the soil around the dahlias free from weeds by regular hoeing. Hoeing also encourages root development.*

the showbench, you may decide that this is acceptable.

But if you need mass support I would recommend the method used by the Dutch growers in their trials and show gardens. Stout stakes are thrust in every 3m (10ft) along the dahlia rows and wires are drawn tightly between them outside the plants, so that they are held safely between the wires. Once the plants start to grow together, they help to support each other too. If you can reduce the time needed to support your dahlias, you will have more time to admire their blooms.

MULCHING

While hoeing towards mid-summer (Fig. 5), you will notice small wisps of white root coming to the surface. This indicates that the feeder roots are spreading rapidly and that you should put the hoe away and take the next step in successful cultivation – mulching the plot. Mulching suppresses weeds and holds moisture in the soil – very important in a dry summer. But if the right materials are used, it also helps feed the plants. Any type of manure, compost or hop manure will do this for you and the natural action of the rain or your own watering will carry nutrients to the dahlias' roots throughout the summer. In fact, a summer mulch can be so successful that feeder roots will rise from the normal soil level and work their way into the mulch. That, believe me, will bring you top class results.

FEEDING

By mid-summer the first buds and blooms will be appearing – especially on the smaller-flowered types. From now on you should be sure to feed your plants regularly. Summer feeding is essential if they are to keep producing good quality blooms. Choose the feed and method of application that best suits you. It could be a liquid fertilizer made by diluting a concentrate and watering this on to the plants' roots from a watering can. Some prefer foliar feeding – spraying the same kind of dilute liquid feed over the leaves from a fine mist sprayer. Or you could broadcast a granular or powdered fertilizer over the ground and leave it for the rain to take it to the plants' roots.

If you have mulched your dahlias, I think it would be best to liquid feed from a watering can (Fig. 6). But if you prefer a granular or powdered feed, I suggest you follow each application with a heavy watering if it does not rain. I would recommend a feed – liquid or otherwise – that is high in nitrogen like Phostrogen, which also has a high potash and phosphate content, the perfectly balanced fertilizer for dahlias. Later in the season you can switch to a

6. *Water new plants at least twice a week until they are fully established.*

liquid feed with a higher potash content to help intensify the dahlias' colouring and, even more important, help their underground tubers develop.

DISBUDDING

As the first blooms form, you might wish to improve their size and quality, whether you are aiming to exhibit at your local show or just want better flowers with longer, stronger stems for your vases. This only calls for a little disbudding – removing some of the surplus buds, a minor act of horticul-

7. *For bigger, better dahlias, a little disbudding is recommended. Remove any side buds early on for longer stems.*

tural surgery that does not harm the plant or impair the production of blooms over the season, while definitely improving growth in mid-season. The tip of each stem on the plant carries three buds, a central or main bud with two much smaller buds set close behind it. To ensure reasonable stems about 60 cm (2 ft) long, remove these smaller buds to leave only the central bud to flower (Fig. 7). You can produce even longer stems, wanted perhaps by an

Opposite: *Ball dahlias are as popular today as they were over one hundred years ago when they were known as Double Show & Fancy dahlias.*

aspiring showman, by removing the shoots from the leaf axils immediately below the bud cluster.

CARE OF BLOOMS

Here are a few tips to help you get the best from your dahlia blooms while they are at their peak. When you cut blooms for vases indoors or for your friends, always do so first thing in the morning – before the sun is up, if possible. After a night's rest, the plants will have restocked with water, so the blooms will not droop. Failing that, cut them late at night and leave the blooms in a deep container of water overnight. *Never* cut dahlias when the sun is on them – that is the quickest way to ensure that the blooms will collapse forthwith.

Dahlias intended for home decoration should be stood in deep water – the taller the vase the better – piercing the hollow stems at several points where they will be immersed. Never stand vases of dahlias in direct sun but keep them as far away from windows as possible. Their brilliant colours will light up the darkest corner of your room. Finally, never be tempted to stand a vase of dahlias on your TV set. If you do, their blooms and foliage will collapse before *News at Ten* is over!

If you are cutting blooms for exhibition, treat them as I have described for cut flowers, but make sure that once cut they are kept in the shade until they appear on the showbench. If the show is nearby, it would be best to arrange them in their vases at home, then carry the vases to the show ready for judging.

Remember that any oversize dahlia blooms are automatically disqualified by the judges, who use special rings to measure them. To avoid the ignominy of a N.A.S. (Not according to schedule) on your entry card, you could obtain a set of these size rings from the N.D.S. Secretary (address elsewhere in this book), who will send them to you for about £4, including postage.

SPECIALIZED CULTIVATION

□ GROWING FOR CUT BLOOMS

If you want to plant dahlias specifically for cut blooms, you should first of all choose varieties that exactly suit this requirement. The smaller-flowered types, like the Miniature and Small Cactus, Semi-Cactus, Decoratives, Balls and Pompons come into this category. I have dealt with their individual characteristics in Chapter 3. Such varieties will yield a host of blooms from the earliest that can be out by mid summer to those that will last right through the summer and autumn until the first severe frost stops them.

Lay out your cut flower plot in long narrow beds as I have described earlier. You could support the plants by using the Dutch growers' method, running wires along either side of the row, stretched between posts. The dahlias' stems will then have a free run to grow perfectly straight and strong – and if disbudded too, long-stemmed and just right for vases and bowls. There is nothing more absurd than offering short-stemmed posies to your friends that would hardly fill a pint-sized jug.

To keep up a steady season-long supply of dahlia blooms it is essential that the plots are never allowed to dry out. It would greatly simplify matters if you could install ground-laid watering lines or overhead sprays which can be switched on whenever the need demands.

Feeding is easily done, and if you want to save time you could attach a device to your watering equipment so that liquid fertilizer is directed where it is most needed, just at the press of a button. You can even protect your dahlia plants against invading insects by using those same spray lines to take insecticide directly to the growing plants. The only thing you have to do yourself these days, it seems, is pick the flowers!

Some dahlia growers go further and cover their cut flower plot to make sure all the blooms are kept pristinely clean. This is certainly a good idea, as a heavy rainstorm or an inconsiderate neighbour with a bonfire could easily spoil your dahlias for a while. But the tent-like wooden framework supporting polythene sheeting that is used is more suitable for a showman than for a gardener who just wants to cut plenty of dahlias for his house.

□ GROWING FOR SHOW

A showman's dahlia garden is something else again. By the very nature of his or her ambitions – there are many first class lady exhibitors – one of the first considerations is that the blooms must be absolutely clean and unblemished, whether from insect attack, bleaching or wilting due to the vagaries of the weather, or distorted in any way. Most showmen consider it essential to cover their valuable crop. But whether or not to cover dahlias intended for show remains a highly contentious matter. Some growers must, others feel compelled to join them because they might lose points if they did not, but there are those who would not besmirch their elegant gardens with a hideous polythene, glass or canvas structure, no matter how certain it made victory.

So just how much value is placed on covers? First of all, the National Dahlia Society, who make the rules for adjudicating dahlias, do not frown on displaying at shows dahlias that have been under cover. Their view is that such flowers enhance a flower show and so the public are able to see dahlias at their very best – a good point. Naturally, covers do not appear in any showman's garden until the buds start to show colour, towards late summer. Polythene sheeting then rises like the morning sun and presents the grower with extra problems.

First is watering. If you cover the garden, you exclude the life-giving rain, so you have the additional chore of providing ample water to maintain full and sustained growth. Remember that at this stage the plants are almost fully grown, with massive leaves and stems, so they demand a great deal of moisture. Besides this, covering the area – and many show people cover their whole garden – raises the overall temperature in which the dahlias grow. So you need to know precisely what is happening to your flowers under the covers as they develop to perfection quite differently from those left out in the open.

Most of our champions today – and some 30 championships are held in the north and south each year – grow their dahlias under cover. I recently wrote a series of articles for a leading gardening newspaper covering the best dahlia growers in Britain, and every one of them had a set of covers, which surely speaks for itself. But protecting the plants with covers is not the only reason exhibitors use these aids.

During the six-week-long show season, during late summer and early autumn, the covers also provide a place for the showman to work, cutting and packing the blooms for show – an awesome task, believe me. The spreading covers protecting the dahlias against the weather now offer similar protection to the grower as he cuts, canes and packs his blooms. Many showmen have large arc-lights fitted in the corners of the structure and it is common to see these dedicated folk working into the small hours cutting blooms, ready to meet a deadline 100 miles or more from home.

☐ GROWING UNDER GLASS

Considering the dahlia's sub-tropical origins, it is surprising that growing these flowers in a greenhouse or conservatory during the summer is not more popular. I suppose most gardeners wish to use their limited area of glass to grow more exotic plants or food crops,

Opposite: *A Miniature Ball, 'Cherida' yields plenty of 8–10 cm (3–4 in) bronze and lilac blooms on 90 cm (3 ft) tall plants.*

Above: *Purple Pompon 'Diana Gregory' is an old variety from Australia, still much favoured by exhibitors.*

or raise summer and autumn plants. Those who do use a greenhouse will tell you that the space should be as large as possible. An average small greenhouse, around 2.4 m × 1.8 m (8 ft × 6 ft), is usually a failure, but larger structures can yield something above average. I have grown exhibition blooms in my own greenhouse, as have many of my contemporaries, planting them in the soil in the ground rather than in pots or tubs.

This means enriching the soil in some way, either preparing it in advance during the autumn while still using the staging above for propagating in spring, or by turning it over and top-dressing it in mid spring, when the dahlias can be safely planted. You will then have both earlier and later flowers, defeating those mid autumn frosts. With no worries about dirty weather, you should have pristine blooms from the very first opening bud.

But there are some snags to take into account. Watering is all-important, as for exhibitors' dahlias under covers in the open garden or those on patios. Higher temperatures have to be catered for too, and it is often necessary to bring a fan or two into operation in high summer to cool the greenhouse. Being in a confined space – and growing in poor light if you have had to shade the house to keep temperatures down – the plants tend to get drawn and develop thin, weak inadequate stems. This is best overcome by experimenting with varieties that do well in such conditions. Note which varieties are grown by the dahlia nurserymen who exhibit at Chelsea Show every spring. All their dahlias are grown under glass and will have been planted very early, in mid to late winter, so they are ready in time for that prestigious show. Getting them to bloom in late spring, two months or more before the normal time is a credit, not only to the grower but to the versatility of these extraordinary flowers.

□ COLLECTING DAHLIAS

Now a word about specialist collectors and growers. I must count myself among these enthusiasts who import dahlias from almost every country in the world where the flower thrives. Parcels of small roots, pot tubers or so-called 'chicken-legs' – a split or division of a larger tuber that looks just like a chicken's leg – reach me from behind the Iron Curtain and all over Europe, from the Americas, Australasia, India, South Africa, Japan – in fact there is hardly a country without a dahlia enthusiast or two within its borders.

The stock that arrives takes many forms, besides the easily recognizable chicken-leg. I have had baby tubers no larger than a thimble that have been coaxed into life and then produced plants as large as a tall shrub. Such activity, delightful as it is, is hardly for the beginner. You need to enjoy growing dahlias in the ordinary way for some years, then specialize, which brings the elements of surprise and achievement and, when some variety from the other side of the world wins for you at a show, great pleasure. And, of course, there is always that feeling of success that you can get by producing a dahlia unknown to your colleagues and competitors!

You have to cater for such arrivals at any time of the year. After all, dahlias are growing in South Africa and the Antipodes when we are more interested in our Christmas turkey! Usually the minute tubers, kept deliberately small to reduce airmail costs, can be coaxed to produce one growth point or eye. I set each tuber in a small seed tray filled with soilless compost. It is soon apparent if the newcomer has taken root, as it will cling tenaciously to the compost after a week or so in a heated greenhouse.

If it arrives in mid or late summer, when my own plants are in bloom, I still use heat to induce growth, but with a heated tray/propagator, checking with a thermometer if temperatures are high outside to make sure the new tubers are not boiled. When growth starts – and failures can be counted on the fingers of one hand, such is the dahlia's vitality – the entire trayful of compost and new tuber is moved into a larger, deeper tray of fresh compost. Here the roots can thrive. After a further two weeks of such luxury, the whole block of compost is carefully removed and planted in the open garden. Such care ensures that when you eventually lift it in the autumn, you are guaranteed a large, ripe tuber from stock received late from overseas which will form the basis of your future stock of that variety.

There are many in our dahlia fraternity who collect dahlias like this, just as others collect stamps or coins. It is a rewarding and pleasurable hobby.

PESTS AND DISEASES

Throughout the dahlia growing season you cannot afford to neglect the perpetual battle against the plants' predators. Dahlias, like other flowers, have a host of enemies which never cease trying to damage our lovely crop. Yet we are well equipped these days to deal with any invader. Let us look at the most important of them and how we can counter their attacks.

□ PESTS

APHIDS   These come in a variety of colours – greenfly, blackfly and colours in between. They are slow-moving and collect on the choicest, most succulent parts of our plants – the new emerging shoots and growing tips. They are an easy target for a contact insecticide, based on malathion, for example. But one sweep over the plants will not be sufficient to keep aphids at bay. They need a regular spraying programme, carried out every seven days to kill those present on the plants and offer an unsavoury dish for others to feed on. Eventually they get the message and seek pastures new.

THRIPS, CAPSIDS AND EARWIGS
This trio is more difficult to control than the aphids, because they are able to dart about among the foliage quite dramatically. In fact, the earwig is equipped with a pair of folding wings that allow it to glide swiftly to safety. The darting thrip, of which the prime example is the amazing leaf hopper, can in fact only be controlled by regular spraying, hence

the need to keep it going to deter if not eliminate them.

The earwig will need more attention. Twice a season, in early summer while our dahlias are young, and again in late summer while they are at the peak of flowering, the earwig produces masses of tiny nymphs which feed on anything green and organic. They can wreak awful damage, so take them very seriously indeed.

You can trap them by placing small inverted clay pots stuffed with straw on top of the supporting canes (Fig. 8). You will find that, after a night's work among your plants, these nocturnal feeders hide away in the dark inside the pots. You can then despatch them in a container of almost neat insecticide or

Above: *'Pensford Marion', a Pompon, originating from Bristol, is a fine bloom that is often staged at shows.*
Opposite: *Cactus dahlias were discovered almost by accident by a Dutch nurseryman in the 1870s. Today they are recognized as ideal for all purposes, but especially cut flower use.*

paraffin. If inclined, you could also use the showman's method of dealing with earwigs. Lightly smear the top few centimetres (inches) of each flower stem to just beneath the bud with Vaseline (petroleum jelly). It sounds messy, but it is not. Simply put a little of the jelly in your hand, then stroke it on the stems. The warm air will spread it so it forms a barrier over which no earwig can pass.

Similarly such barriers will also prove useful in deterring caterpillars.

8. *Trap earwigs by placing pots stuffed with straw on the support cane. Dispose of the pots' contents each morning.*

9. *Slugs and snails can be repelled by baiting the dahlia plot with pellets or cream containing metaldehyde.*

SLUGS AND SNAILS   You would think that slugs and snails with their ponderous ways would pose no problem at all. But they can and do, especially in late spring, soon after planting. Worst of all, perhaps, are the very tiny slugs that can bare a stem overnight, while snails can cut through a leaf in a trice, leaving only a stem which never recovers from such a vicious attack. To combat these molluscs, use slug bait or, if the problem is extensive, a liquid slug killer (Fig. 9). The bait is made of compressed bran impregnated with the chemical metaldehyde, lethal but happily also irresistible to slugs.

These too are night feeders. After a night among your plants, feeding on the bran, they expire in the open, ready for you to clear them away. If you have a serious slug problem, you can dilute liquid metaldehyde in water and apply it straight on the soil around your plants with a watering can. The effect is quite dramatic – slugs seem to disappear overnight. Regular waterings with this mixture will keep your plot free all the summer.

RED SPIDER MITE I have left the worst pest until last. This predator, which is in fact neither a spider nor really red, can hardly be seen with the naked eye, yet it masses on the plants' lower leaves, killing them off and then gradually moving upwards until the whole plant is ruined. There is no cure for a serious red spider invasion, so you must burn the plants that have deteriorated too badly. To spot the mites early, watch for any yellowing of the lower leaves or any paling of the normal healthy green. Remove these at once and burn them, then soak the area they came from with a heavy dose of insecticide; malathion is recommended.

□ DISEASES

Fortunately these are not too prevalent among dahlias. The worst you are likely to experience is virus infection among your plants. The most common virus disease is known as **dahlia mosaic**, easily spotted as the leaves tend to yellow along the veins (the mosaic) and blister on the reverse. Besides this, some plants' growth is cramped and they refuse to grow more than 30cm (1ft) high – hence the name **stunt virus** for this trouble. There is no cure for stunt or any other virus that cripples dahlias. So if you spot an infected plant, remove it immediately, as it is a danger to other, healthy plants, and burn it.

Dahlias can occasionally be affected by fungus diseases during the growing season, the most prevalent being **dahlia wilt**. A form of *Botrytis cinerea* (black rot) will attack the bases of the stems in damp conditions. Once it has taken

10. *In mid-autumn lift your tubers whether there has been a frost or not. Avoid undue damage to the larger roots by lifting with a spade rather than a fork.*

hold, it spreads upwards quite rapidly until the whole plant wilts and collapses. If you notice some of the lower leaves of a plant are wilting, showing the fungus is present, then spray at once with a benomyl-based fungicide, which will remedy the situation.

I hope that all this talk of predators and diseases will not make you over-anxious. You must always keep a watchful eye for trouble, but in most seasons the majority of dahlia growers do not even glimpse any of these invaders – forewarned is forearmed, however.

LIFTING AND STORAGE

Above: *Small Cactus 'Klankstad Kerkrade' is still one of the finest dahlias ever raised after three decades of exhibition and garden success.*
Opposite: *'De Sarasate': The value of this Dutch beauty, a Large Semi-cactus, is in its rich, deep colouring. Though a Large it provides plenty of blooms.*

Cultivation comes full circle with the arrival of autumn and the first killer frost. You will certainly have had a full and rewarding season by the time it arrives, but before you dare take it easy for a few weeks until the cycle of work starts all over again, you need to extricate the tubers from the soil, cleaning and storing them carefully for the winter.

Some gardeners will tell you that it is unnecessary to lift the tubers for the winter. But there are, in fact, only a few parts of Britain where winters are normally mild enough for the roots to remain outdoors. It takes only one bad winter though – possible in favoured areas as well as the normally cold ones – for you to lose every tuber you have. Much safer to lift them and have a reasonable chance of enjoying another season's display from your dahlias.

Once their foliage has been blackened, the tubers can be lifted from the dahlia plot with a spade or fork and taken under cover to be cleaned (Fig. 10). First remove as much of the adher-

11. *Prepare your tubers for winter storage by reducing the amount of old root and stem. Trim off the surplus or 'hairlike' roots, and cut back the old stem to an inch or two in length.*

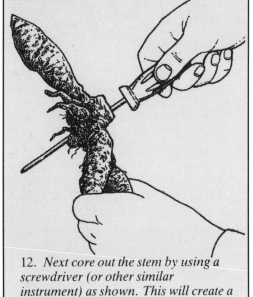

12. *Next core out the stem by using a screwdriver (or other similar instrument) as shown. This will create a perfect drainage hole.*

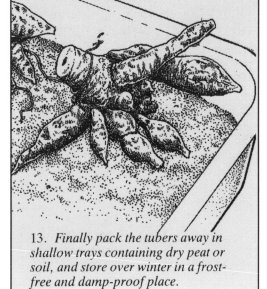

13. *Finally pack the tubers away in shallow trays containing dry peat or soil, and store over winter in a frost-free and damp-proof place.*

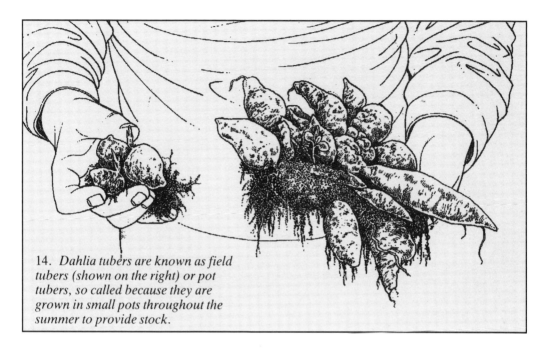

14. *Dahlia tubers are known as field tubers (shown on the right) or pot tubers, so called because they are grown in small pots throughout the summer to provide stock.*

ing soil as you can, then, using secateurs, remove any surplus roots up to 0.6cm (¼in) thick, leaving only the really fat, bulky parts. Next cut down the stem, leaving only 2.5cm (1in) or so protruding above the cluster of tubers (Fig. 11). Then thrust a screwdriver or drill down through the centre of the root to emerge on the other side (Fig. 12). This drainage hole you have created will release any surplus water trapped in the centre of the tubers and after a few more days on the greenhouse staging to dry thoroughly, your whole collection of dahlia tubers can be dipped in a benomyl fungicide. This will go a long way towards preventing losses from fungus attack while they are in store.

Finally, pack the tubers away in shallow trays of dry peat or soil, where they can overwinter safely (Fig. 13). Find a frost-free damp-proof spot and look over the roots about once a fortnight to make sure they are still healthy. If any show signs of mildew or botrytis, clean them up, treat them again with benomyl and return them to store.

If you are going to propagate from the overwintered roots, you will be taking them out of store in late winter (Fig. 14). If on the other hand you do not need them until spring for replanting or dividing (see chapter on propagation), continue to examine them regularly and attend to their needs as they arise.

Now if you look out on the bare plot from which you have just taken your dahlia roots, you will see that it is precisely the scene with which we started. Another season begins.

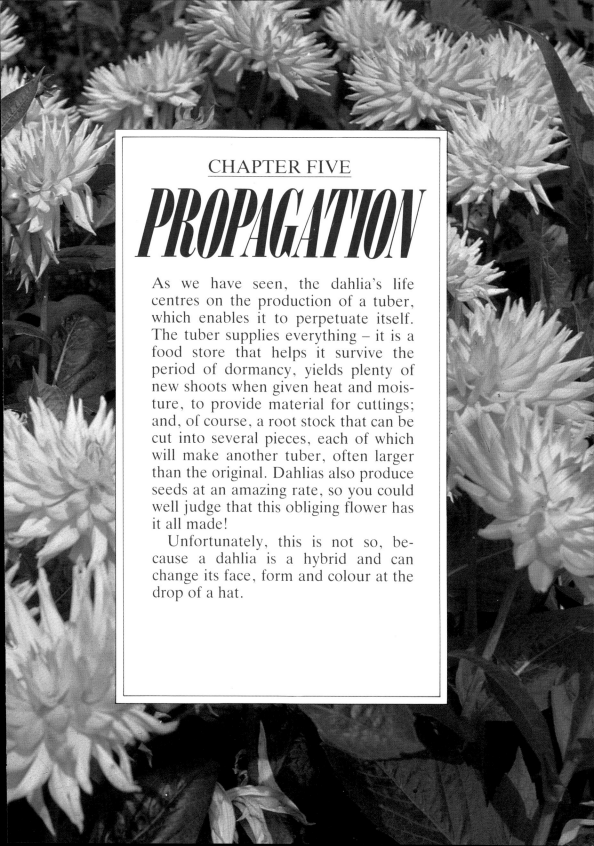

CHAPTER FIVE

PROPAGATION

As we have seen, the dahlia's life centres on the production of a tuber, which enables it to perpetuate itself. The tuber supplies everything – it is a food store that helps it survive the period of dormancy, yields plenty of new shoots when given heat and moisture, to provide material for cuttings; and, of course, a root stock that can be cut into several pieces, each of which will make another tuber, often larger than the original. Dahlias also produce seeds at an amazing rate, so you could well judge that this obliging flower has it all made!

Unfortunately, this is not so, because a dahlia is a hybrid and can change its face, form and colour at the drop of a hat.

If you save seeds from a dahlia plant, the progeny that result are almost always far removed in appearance from their parent. So if you want to reproduce a scarlet Pompon you admired in a friend's garden, you can only obtain a replica by growing a cutting from the original root or from part of it. There are some seeds that reproduce exactly to form and plant height, but they are confined to bedding varieties whose blooms have open (single) centres and the basic six petals. Though there has been some improvement of late, seed-raised dahlias are still an uncertain quantity. Their colours cannot be guaranteed, so it is necessary to find other methods of propagating this exciting flower.

If seeds are not the answer, just how do you increase the stock of dahlias you have in your garden? There are, in fact, two methods. The first is to take cuttings. To do this the overwintered tubers must be introduced to warmth, light and moisture early in the year. Having been kidded that spring has arrived, they throw a whole mass of shoots from the crown of the root, where the old stem joins the fattened parts of the tuber. These shoots are encouraged to grow in the greenhouse by feeding and watering, and as they reach an acceptable size, about 8–10 cm (3–4 in) long, they are severed from the parent tuber. Then they are induced to grow roots by using special rooting mixtures in a propagating box or frame.

Once rooted, the cuttings have become plants and are potted individually in pots of good compost. When suffi-ciently developed, they are set out in the garden to produce full-sized plants which bear masses of blooms that season. That same cutting will also develop a strong tuber that will continue the cycle of growth just like the original. The dahlia trade is based on this method of rooting cuttings, producing many millions throughout the world that go part way to satisfying the dahlia lovers' insatiable demand.

While the dahlia nurseryman needs to raise masses of plants like this to maintain his business, the third method of propagation is more to the liking of the amateur. I should judge – there are no statistics to prove it – replanting complete overwintered tubers, and using splits or divisions of them, is by far the more popular method of propagation. Let us look more closely at these three methods of increasing dahlias.

FROM SEEDS

As I have said, sowing seeds has a limited appeal to the dahlia enthusiast, unless he or she is aiming to produce new varieties, a subject dealt with elsewhere. Seed sowing can only be relied upon to raise the simple low-growing, single-centred varieties. Even these have no guaranteed colour, so you sow your seed and your choice is made for you. The seed specialists do offer seeds of various sorts, but they do not profess to have cracked the centuries' old problem of growing replicas of the classic forms. You will see Pompon seed or Decorative seed offered, but most of the offspring will be open-centred or at best, semi-double. You will get an occasional fully double bloom, but these are the exception rather than the rule. The day is yet to come when you will be able to buy a packet of seed that gives you 50 plants of a fully double yellow Cactus, that will grow to the cut flower height of 90cm (3ft) or more. However, many gardeners are content with the product of seed-sown dahlias. If you are one, this is the way to obtain seedlings.

Sowing, whether for bedding dahlias or other kinds, can take place in late winter or early spring in a heated greenhouse. If you wish, you could sow in mid to late spring in an unheated frame, but blooming will then be considerably delayed. Sow in shallow trays and as dahlia seeds are so large and easy to handle, space them out 2.5cm (1in) or so apart. Cover the trays with a sheet of glass and over that a sheet of newspaper, removing both each morning so that the glass can be wiped free from condensation and turned. Germination is speedy and within seven to ten days your first seedlings will be breaking surface. When you see them, remove the glass and cover and allow them to enjoy some light and air. On warm days, spray them overhead morning and night with tepid water.

You will soon be able to handle the newcomers and can move them from the seed tray in which they have germinated to deeper trays or 8cm (3in) pots. I use Levington (soilless) compost for this move, and transfer them to a cooler part of the greenhouse. Here they will thrive, and by mid to late spring you will have some sturdy young plants that can

be moved into a cold frame to harden off before being asked to endure the outdoor conditions. No seedlings, whether used as bedding plants in your borders or simply to enhance your garden must be planted out until all fear of frost is over. Just a few degrees of frost will damage or even kill off young, tender seedlings. Plants damaged like this rarely recover completely and will perform poorly.

Once safely planted out and established, the seedlings will develop early blooms, a great advantage. They can even flower in the frames before being planted in the garden. A first-year seedling will also form a fine tuber in a single summer, emulating the rooted cutting and split tuber. But the advantages of this are small, since the same result can be obtained the next season by sowing seeds again, which makes saving tubers from these plants superfluous.

FROM CUTTINGS

Some dahlia lovers consider raising plants from rooted cuttings early in the year a fascinating pastime which, they tell me, gives them as much satisfaction as creating the blooms themselves. I would certainly agree that it is satisfying raising a whole range of young plants from the gnarled and withered-looking tubers taken from store in late winter. Perhaps it is the miracle of re-birth that is so fascinating, but whatever the reason raising young plants from cuttings certainly brings considerable pleasure and pride.

A start is usually made in late winter, although it is possible to start later than this. Starting early does offer the advantage of a shorter storage period for the roots, with less risk of losses from fungus attack. There will also be a wider selection of plants in various stages of development to choose from when planting out and, best of all, early flowers from some of the larger plants created. The main disadvantage would seem to be the extra cost of heating your greenhouse, but if this is divided among the other plants you are raising, such as annuals, bulbs, early tomatoes and cucumbers, it is not as bad as it first appears.

□ START THE TUBERS
To start with, carefully examine the tubers taken from store for any signs of damage. Pare away dry rot from the fleshy roots with a sharp knife and cauterize the wounds with a good fungicide such as benomyl. When any wounds you have made have healed, the doctored roots and the completely healthy ones can be plunged into shallow trays of compost (Fig. 15). Levington soilless compost is ideal, or you could use an equal parts mixture of peat and loam or other open compost that holds moisture well. By plunging, I mean pushing the roots into the surface of the mix rather than burying them. Set the tubers so that the crown, where the old stem joins the fattened parts of the root, is just above the surface of the compost. The reason for this is that most new growth starts from the crown, and if buried it could well start to rot.

It is best not to water boxed tubers, so ensure that the mixture is well moistened before they are boxed. If you can maintain a night temperature in late winter and early spring of around 10°C (50°F), the first new shoots will appear as bright red and green eyes. At this point you can water the compost, but still avoid the crowns if possible. Given reasonable weather, with bright sunny early spring days, it will take only a week or so for these eyes to elongate to around 8–10cm (3–4in), perfect for making cuttings (Fig. 16).

At this stage you should prepare some form of propagating frame or box that can be set on your staging over the heat source. Or you could fix a soil-warming cable inside a propagator to provide the ideal environment for rooting. A lidded or hinged frame, a little taller at the back than at the front so condensation drains away, is easy to make or you could buy a plastic domed propagating case, perhaps with its own built-in heat source. Having selected your propagator, spread a few inches of moist peat over the base and stand small trays of rooting mixture on this. The rooting mixture should be open in texture, a favourite with dahlia growers being an equal parts mix of peat and coarse potting grit or sand. Moisten and rub these ingredients together, then firm them well into the containers. Test its firmness by inserting a pencil in the mix. If you can give the pencil a half-turn and

Opposite: 'Inca Dambuster', a Semi-cactus, is one of the largest dahlias ever raised in Britain, reaching bloom widths of 37.5–40cm (15–16in).

15. *In late winter old tubers can be stimulated into growth by maintaining an overnight temperature of about 10°C.*

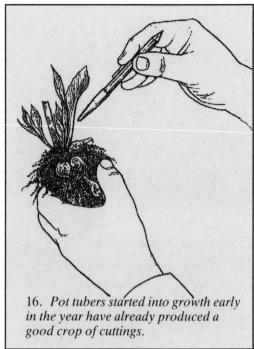

16. *Pot tubers started into growth early in the year have already produced a good crop of cuttings.*

it comes out clean, leaving a neat hole, your rooting compost is ready to receive the first batch of cuttings.

□ **TAKE THE CUTTINGS**
Remove the cuttings from the parent root carefully, bearing in mind that if some of them fail to root, you will need further cuttings to replace them. So sever each cutting fractionally above where it emerges from the crown (Fig. 17). This will leave a growth base from which other cuttings will quickly develop. Some gardeners insist that cuttings should be snapped or bent away from the crown, taking away the entire growth base. They are supposed to be easier to root, but I have never found

this to be so. Anyway, the number of cuttings obtainable from that root would be very limited, and if your first batch of cuttings failed, you would lose the whole stock.

When you have collected a batch of cuttings ready for rooting, trim the base of each one, just below a node, where the embryo leaves join the main stem, and dip them in a rooting powder or liquid. I have not noticed any significant difference in the time taken to root between the powder and the liquid. After coating the bottom 2.5 cm (1 in) or so of each cutting insert them neatly about 2.5 cm (1 in) deep into the trays of prepared rooting mixture. Put the lid or cover on the propagating frame or box

17. *Sever cuttings from the tuber when they are about 8-10 cm (3-4 in) long. Use a sharp knife and take the cutting fractionally above the point where it emerges from the tuber.*

and shade it from bright sunlight immediately (Fig. 18). Bright sun or even a bright, hazy day can cause unshaded cuttings to wilt, after which it is extremely difficult to get them to stand upright again. To encourage quick rooting, spray the cuttings morning and evening with warm, clear water. Remove the frame-lid every day and wipe away any condensed moisture.

Taking these few, sensible steps will avoid one of the major dangers with rooting dahlia cuttings – damping off, a fungus infection that starts by blackening the base of the cutting and then spreads upwards to destroy it completely. If left unchecked, the trouble will spread right through your propagator. If you see early signs of infection, you can help prevent its spread by allowing a little more air into your frame, propping open the lid or cover a fraction.

□ POT THEM UP

You will soon know that your dahlia cuttings have developed roots by the way they stand perkily upright and, when gently tugged, cling tenaciously to the rooting medium. When this happens, remove them from the propagator and give them something more substantial to feed on than the barren peat and sand in which they have rooted! Pot on or box the new plants in soilless compost or, if you prefer, John Innes potting compost No 1 (Fig. 19). I use the soilless

18. *Using a modern propagator is the most efficient way to root cuttings. Insert cuttings about 2.5 cm (1 in) into the compost.*

19. *When the cuttings have rooted, they should be moved into small pots or trays containing good potting compost.*

mix which I find is easy to handle and keep watered and is thoroughly reliable. Once you have potted the rooted cuttings, they can be moved away from the warmer part of the greenhouse where they have rooted to a cooler position where they can grow on steadily. It pays to shade the freshly potted cuttings for a day or two to ensure that they do not wilt.

If you start taking your cuttings in early to mid spring, which is the usual time, then by the end of this period you will have some very strong, healthy plants bursting with energy. To consolidate this growth, move the plants or boxes into a cold frame, where they can stay for several weeks to harden off

ready for planting in the open garden as spring ends and summer begins. During their time in frames you could find that the small pots in which you initially potted the rooted cuttings are now too small for the strong growing plants. A paling of the lower leaves from a dark, healthy green to a sickly shade will indicate this. This requires immediate attention, and if you tap the plants out of the pots, you will discover that they are probably root-bound, with a web of white roots winding around the inside of the pots, having exhausted the compost

Opposite: *'Turbo', an elegant Medium Semi-cactus of recent release from Holland, where so many good new dahlias originate.*

of nutrients. You can remedy this by moving the plant into a larger container, a 13–15cm (5–6in) pot, using the same type of compost as before.

If your plants were exceptionally early, which is quite possible in a good early spring when the weather is favourable, your plants could even exhaust the nutrients provided in the larger pots. Once more there will be a paling or yellowing of the lower foliage. You can easily overcome this problem by giving each cóntainer a half-strength liquid feed at every other watering. By late spring, as planting out time gets near, you will be able to leave the frame lights off altogether on most nights. By now your plants will make you proud as they fill your cold frame with their robust dark green leaves, a sight to gladden the heart of any dahlia devotee.

FROM TUBERS AND DIVISIONS

The third way of propagating dahlias is by using the old tubers, the favourite method among amateurs. After all, a well-grown dahlia root that has been looked after during the winter can give three or four plants of that variety, so if a number of roots are overwintered satisfactorily, there will be enough for the average garden. If you just want to repeat the previous season's display, the tuber can be used without any interference – replanting it as it was lifted. But I would not recommend this, as vigour and quality are more likely to be maintained when a fresh root system is grown from divisions. After all, if you divide

an old root into four pieces, you are creating four separate root systems, each of which can easily reach maximum size and that just has to be four times better than an individed root. Dividing the tubers also saves you a fair amount of heating, because while the best divisions are started under glass, there is no need to begin as early as with cuttings. Mid-spring is quite early enough. Or you can just use a cold frame and start the divisions in late spring without any heating costs at all. If you prefer greenhouse-raised divisions, box up the roots in mid-spring and make sure that night temperatures keep out any frosts. Shallow trays are excellent for starting the overwintered roots in soil and warmth (Fig. 20). Once again, plunge the tubers rather than bury them. With average temperatures higher than when plunging tubers to develop cuttings, you will find that the growth eyes appear rather more quickly.

When the first signs of life appear, you need to act as quickly as possible, as you should divide the tubers while the growths are small, rather than allow them to elongate into proper shoots. Some growers disagree with this, preferring to handle fair-sized shoots rather than eyes. But I believe that, caught this early, the split or division settles into its new quarters far more quickly than if it were left.

□ DIVIDE THEM
Once the eyes have developed, take the whole root from its tray and stand it on a bed of peat or soil. Next, take a sharp knife or small hand saw and cut down

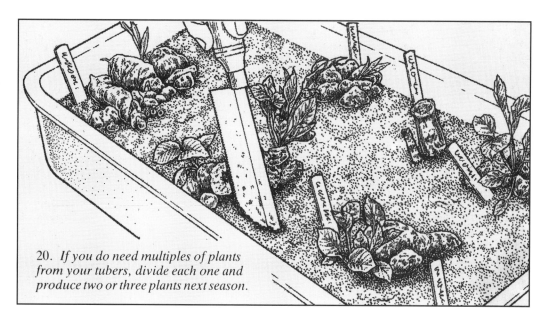

20. *If you do need multiples of plants from your tubers, divide each one and produce two or three plants next season.*

through the centre of the old stem, between the two most prominent eyes of the tuber. This will immediately give you two divisions and you can now see clearly if these can be further sub-divided. There must be an eye and some of the old root on each piece that you separate.

The value of early division is that all the splits you have made can be re-planted in deeper trays of good compost and after further growth lifted out and further sub-divided. If you are a little patient and a bit green-fingered this split–grow–split technique can give you a dozen or more divisions from a well-branched tuber.

Once you have decided that you have enough divisions from your tubers, make sure they have plenty of root room so they can grow successfully. They will continue to need a little heat

for a week or two so that root develop-ment (much slower than on cuttings) is given every chance to flourish. Strong top growth will indicate that you are getting results. When you can see that they have a hold on the new container, they can be moved into a cold frame to harden off alongside the rooted cut-tings. Divisions seldom exhaust the nu-trients available in the deeper trays or boxes, but if this should happen, as indicated by a paling or yellowing of the lower leaves, you can water them with a liquid fertilizer at half strength, just as for the young cuttings.

If you have no equipment to handle divisions – that is the possession of a greenhouse or a coldframe, then all hope is not lost, you merely need to keep the old roots in store until late spring, when they can be split as ex-tracted. Often you will find that tubers

Opposite: *'Wootton Impact', a first-rate Medium Semi-cactus. Given an award at Wisley trials for garden use and an excellent show variety.*
Above: *'Akita' comes from Japan and is referred to as the Chrysanthemum-flowered dahlia, which it patently resembles. In Britain it is included with the Miscellaneous types (Group 10).*

have offered growth points or 'eyes' whilst in storage, and if some of these have elongated (as often happens with potato tubers), then carefully cut away the surplus growth, making sure that the base of the 'eye' is left. Next, cut into as many pieces as you can, again ensuring that the growth point is present on each portion. Just one 'eye' will be enough to produce a normal-sized dahlia bush and a full crop of blooms.

As suggested, late spring (or even a little later as circumstances allow) is perfect for this operation, and the divisions can be planted out in the garden immediately. Provide a base of good, well-rotted compost or peat on which the pieces can rest, and set the growth point approximately 10cm (4in) below the surrounding soil level. Given good weather conditions the first shoots will emerge from the soil at the end of Spring, usually too late to be damaged by frost. However, should frost still be lingering, you can cover up the vulnerable green shoots and leaves by hoeing soil around them (as you would with early potatoes). Any slight miscalculation, which might mean that a sizeable amount of foliage was clear of the soil before those frosts had disappeared, could be countered by covering, at night only of course, with large pots, boxes or even with a few sheets of ordinary newspaper, removing such covering as soon as the sun was up each morning. There is a distinct advantage to the ordinary gardener in the early planting of tubers or divided tubers in this way. Firstly, and most importantly I would suggest, is the fact that you will get much earlier dahlia blooms than you would from rooted cuttings or even seed-raised types. Additionally a dahlia plant created from a split or whole tuber will almost always guarantee another fully developed root for lifting in the autumn – not always the case with rooted cuttings!

□ **PLANTING OUT**

When planting out time arrives, a little extra care is needed as the roots of the divisions in their deeper trays often become entangled and need to be disentangled. You could avoid this by putting each split or division in its own, large pot, but this can be rather expensive and take up a lot of room in your greenhouse. As each piece is teased out from the container, settle it on to a bed of peat or soilless compost at the base of the marker cane (see chapter on cultivation). Position it so that the new top growth is breaking the surface but the whole of the tuber cluster is well below soil level.

By providing a bed of peat or compost under the split, you are encouraging essential root growth and you will find that your tuber divisions will soon race away to be in flower well before the rooted cuttings. This is well known among dahlia growers, and exhibitors use it to provide blooms they might need for the earlier shows in mid to late summer – even for the giant or larger flowered types, for major summer shows like Shrewsbury or Southport. And for gardeners interested in cut flowers, how useful to have dahlias available two or three weeks earlier than normal? On the other hand, it is a fact that dahlias raised from cuttings are more consistent than those from tubers and continue yielding quality blooms much longer into the season.

PROTECT FROM PESTS AND DISEASES

In all of these forms of propagation, whether rooted cuttings, young seed-raised plants or those faithful divisions, keep a careful watch at all times against the influx of predators or diseases. Virus diseases, already discussed in the chapter on cultivation, can show up at any time and in any situation. They are insect-borne, so any sap-sucking insect can attack a plant that is carrying the virus and then move on to a healthy plant and infect it with the poisoned sap.

It is also said that virus can be spread on garden knives and similar tools when taking cuttings, which is quite possible, though there has never been much evidence to prove it.

It is quite possible to store the tuber of an infected plant through the winter without realizing it is unhealthy and then, when re-introduced to warmth and water, clearly see the symptoms of disease. New shoot growth could be stunted, new leaves twisted away from the vertical and the veins and margins of the leaves pale or yellowing. If you notice such symptoms, take out the whole root and burn it. Its presence is a grave danger to the rest of your stock.

Great care must be taken during all stages of propagation to keep down insect predators. Regularly spray in the greenhouse and cold frame, in whose closely confined space you should also lift and spray underneath the leaves, where aphids in particular gather in unhealthy clusters. Lay bait for earwigs, slugs and snails too, although the former, and to a great extent the latter, give little trouble in the early stages.

If you keep to these few simple rules, there is no reason why you should not be able to obtain a collection of fine, healthy dahlia plants. Whether they have developed from seedlings, cuttings or tuber divisions you will have gained much pleasure and satisfaction from producing them.

CHAPTER SIX

RAISING NEW VARIETIES

Raising new dahlia varieties has never been a problem, even for an average gardener. Unlike some of our other popular flowers, the dahlia does not demand the usual hybridizing paraphernalia, with its camel-hair brushes, pollen interchange, covered seedheads and years of waiting. The dahlia was already a hybrid when it was discovered centuries ago in Central America by the first Spanish settlers there. Since then hardly a year can have passed without the appearance of hundreds of new and different dahlias.

Today, some 200 years after the dahlia's arrival in Europe, the trials lists, commercial catalogues and analyses of specialist dahlia societies are filled each year with the names of novelties that have just been introduced for sale, been winning on showbenches in Britain, the Americas or the Antipodes or have perhaps given a medal-winning performance at a prestigious trial like that conducted at Wisley Garden (Surrey) under the auspices of the Royal Horticultural Society and the National Dahlia Society.

WHAT IS WORTHWHILE?

To provide such a dazzling succession of novelties, we need to be able to raise plenty of new dahlias easily, which is exactly what we do. We also need to know the value of a new dahlia. After all, you could have a beautiful seedling in your garden that is greatly admired by your family, but unless it appeals to others beyond your garden, there would be little mileage in it. So what market or group of people should a prospective dahlia raiser aim for?

Currently, the best sellers are those that find their way into the catalogues of commercial nurserymen, especially on the Continent and in America. A novelty of value can command a reasonable price in a Dutch trader's catalogue, say, as he will be selling to most European countries and further afield. Apart from minor exchanges, mostly between amateurs, there is little other import/export trade and virtually none from this country. Some limitations are imposed on the import and export of tubers or plants by a particular country's tight regulations framed to stop the spread of viruses or other plant diseases that might seriously affect the health of many other plants besides dahlias. The Netherlanders, with their very live and cooperative Ministry of Agriculture, aware that the export of things horticultural is vital to their economy, appear to make life easier for their traders, who export many millions of pounds' worth of plant products each year.

So what do *they* look for in a new dahlia? Well, as dahlia columnist for Britain's No 1 weekly gardening periodical for the last 30 years I have been concerned with the new dahlia varieties. I can tell you there is *no* secret pattern. Beauty is in the eye of the customer! Last year, as I have done for three decades, I took a party of 45 dahlia enthusiasts on a tour of the Dutch dahlia nurseries. At one, near Heemstede, they saw a superb show garden containing some 300 varieties. After a couple of hours they had between them ordered some 200 tubers in some 50 varieties. The nurseryman had stocked his garden well, with the latest bicolors from Germany and Belgium, several elegant new Collerettes in fresh colour breaks, and his speciality, some of the world's best Pompons, imported from Australia, Britain and America, then offered for re-sale to the countries they came from – a slick bit of commerce.

It would seem, therefore, that what appeals is anything eye-catching and floriferous. Striking colours, particularly mixed colours like the variegated kinds and those with colour suffusions (one hue overlaid with another) always sell well to the ordinary gardener. And as most traders know, a good exhibition dahlia, of prizewinning form, can always command a fair price, above the average, in its early years of introduction.

QUALITY SEED PARENTS

So how does one go about breaking into this tight world of new dahlias? Well, firstly, if you want to raise anything worthwhile you must start with a quality collection yourself from which you can later harvest seeds. It is a known fact that open-centred (single-flowered) varieties like the bedding types or the Collerettes inhibit the production of double-flowered types. Bees and insects or even a fair wind moving pollen from a single variety to a potential double, can turn the latter's seedlings into a poor conglomeration of singles, of little use to anyone. So grow only the best varieties you can get and grow them compactly in small beds well away from other varieties, like the singles, that might affect them.

This pattern has been followed over the years by many famous raisers. By block planting the type or types you are aiming for and excluding any interference from 'foreign' pollen, the resulting seeds should include something of value. The seeds should be allowed to mature fully on the plant, so the best and ripest seeds that can be obtained in our very fickle climate are those formed by the very first blooms to appear, in midsummer. These are left to form

seedheads by late summer, or even helped to do so by removing any lingering petals by hand to reveal the familiar cone-shaped seed head.

By early autumn these can be collected from the plants with a short length of stem attached, so they can be stood in water under cover in the greenhouse for a few more weeks to ripen fully. Later, the seeds are taken from the seedhead and stored in small, tight-lidded tins.

Once they have been sown and set out in the garden, it remains only for you, the raiser, to select any of the new arrivals that show promise. Many dahlia lovers who like raising new varieties will plant out two, three or five thousand seedlings in the hope that there might be just one or two worth keeping. This may seem a giant waste of time and space, but it occasionally offers a 'pearl in the oyster'. If you think this practice is only suitable for amateurs, you would be wrong. Many professionals I know do exactly this, including some of Holland's top raisers of new varieties whom I have met over the years. (At one time a dahlia nurseryman in Holland would think nothing of introducing 50 novelties in his catalogue every year). They would walk among the beds of seedling dahlias and casually uproot anything growing there that displeased them. Anything that showed a hint of promise or, as one friend expressed it, 'had the smell of commerce' would be carefully tagged with a series of stars – one indicating it should be kept for a second look the next season, up to four for something exceptional.

CHERISH NEW STOCK

'Jescot Julie' classified as Miscellaneous Flowered, is officially known as a Double-Flowered Orchid dahlia!

Having found something that holds promise, you need to remember that the tuber the seedling produces is the only means by which the newcomer can be perpetuated. So the root needs to be carefully treated while in store until it can produce cuttings to ensure plenty of stock. After two years, it will be shown at trials or perhaps entered in top seedling classes where, if given a good reception by dahlia enthusiasts, it will be offered for sale. The same pattern is followed by the amateur who is raising new dahlias.

If a seedling dahlia pleases, it is offered to the governing committee for selection and then, if successful, shown to the public on several trial grounds. Blooms are also entered in the many top seedling classes held each year by the National Dahlia Society and other top specialist groups, and the winners become famous, so they are wanted by dahlia lovers everywhere. The results of shows and trials in this country become urgent reading for dahlia lovers overseas, and vice-versa, and an enthusiast intent on improving his or her collection of exhibition or cut flower varieties also becomes a customer, seeking out new dahlias.

'Tohsuikyoh' is from Japan as its name implies.
Yet another Miscellaneous form that is normally
referred to as Orchid-flowered.

Occasionally, a new dahlia, particularly in the exhibition world, is really outstanding and an amateur raiser will seek a nurseryman's help to distribute the stock to customers. It is then usual for the raiser to receive payment, averaging some 50 per cent of the net sales figure in the first year, but a smaller percentage in succeeding years. Such transactions are a matter of negotiation between the amateur and the professional, so the better known or more skilful raiser can often obtain better terms.

You will see then that raising new dahlias is largely a gamble, though you need to know the market and the dahlia scene. However, having said that, I must pay tribute to many dedicated dahlia enthusiasts, almost all amateurs, who still persist with logging parents, sorting out the first class seed-makers and believing deeply in Mendel's genetic laws. Their object is to bring together the best aspects of the pairs of dahlias they are crossing to produce the perfect dahlia which they hope will contain the best qualities of both. Their efforts may not be any better than those achieved by the random seedling grower but they do contribute to the overall pattern of new introductions which still, despite a plethora of pollen movement and records often going back decades, have to contend with the fact that this flower is a veteran hybridizer that will, in the end, have its own way.

SPORTS OR MUTATIONS

One of the most successful methods of introducing a new dahlia variety is through securing a sport, or mutation, to give it its correct horticultural name. Sports arise when a bloom of a different colour appears on a plant of an established variety – say a bright yellow suddenly flowering on a normally red-flowered plant. Mutations can also occur in the form of the dahlia, with a Decorative plant throwing a Cactus flower. When the change of colour or form occurs on a successful cut flower or top show variety, the value of such sports is greatly increased.

Nowadays the lists are littered with sports of all sorts. No sooner does a dahlia achieve fame than a colour sport of it occurs. There are numerous examples of this, like the long-serving 'Klankstad Kerkrade', a pale yellow Cactus with a tremendous record of wins over the last 30 years. It has yielded a whole family of mutations in white, rose, pink, lilac and so on, every one successful because of its aristocratic origin. Perhaps the supreme example is the Semi-cactus 'Symbol', another that has been at the top for several decades. It has so many sports, such as salmon, peach and amber, that even keen dahlia enthusiasts confuse them. However, such sports are held in high regard simply because they are always as successful as the parent.

INCREASE FROM CUTTINGS

I know from experience the delight at spotting something different on one of your dahlia plants. One's instinct is to isolate it immediately, but nine out of ten sports are of little value. Only when they occur on a well-known variety will they be considered by anyone outside your garden. If one of worth does appear and the whole plant sports, it is easy to lift and take care of the tuber, take cuttings from it the next spring and hope that when you plant them out the change will prove permanent. A change that affects a whole plant will almost certainly hold, but where only a single branch mutates, you need to take cuttings from that part of the plant as soon as you notice the sport. You can usually take up to half a dozen good cuttings if the sport is seen early in the season. These should be rooted and potted on and grown in heat through the winter (with the help of a nurseryman friend) so you can take more cuttings during the spring from the stock you have established. The next summer will confirm or deny your find. If you are lucky, all your cuttings will be of the new colour break.

One of the most neglected aspects of a sporting dahlia is that relating to form. Almost without exception, gardeners look for a change of colour when contemplating the occurrence of a sport. With the dahlia, a Cactus can alter its form to become a Decorative or Semi-cactus formation; a single-flowered variety can produce a fully double-flowered bloom and the ball varieties can miniaturize themselves, as they did when first discovered in Germany, to become a pompon!

So narrow are the size limits, that here, too, a small-flowered dahlia can promote itself to the medium section by adding a few inches to its bloom size! It is not unknown for the medium blooms to become giant sized in this way.

Your sport can be publicized in the same ways as new seed-raised dahlias, through trials and shows. You will find that separate classes for sports rather than seedlings are included nowadays, particularly at top levels. An unusual colour or form change that arises from an established dahlia variety has a better chance of being recognized by the fraternity than the seed-raised one.

Among the new dahlias that I review each year for the gardening press is a batch of sports – many international but always some from Britain.

One of the pleasures of raising new dahlias, whether from seed or sports is that you, as raiser, can name them. I have raised many new dahlias over the years and named them after my wife, three sons, daughters-in-law, all of my grandchildren and, even my old dog Sandy. None were world beaters, though, and I am still awaiting a blue one so that I can retire to the West Indies! Meanwhile, like so many others, I get a great deal of pleasure out of seedlings, and who knows, I *could* find that pearl one day.

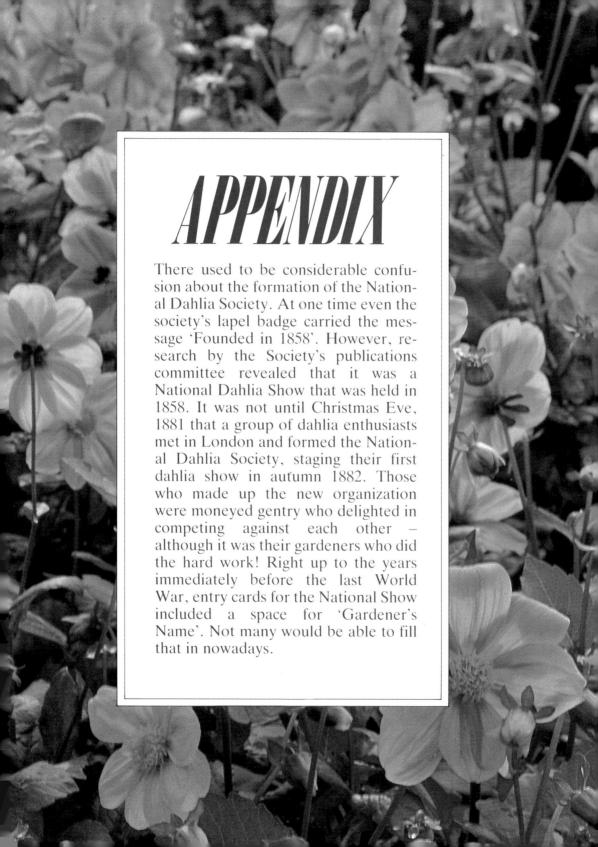

APPENDIX

There used to be considerable confusion about the formation of the National Dahlia Society. At one time even the society's lapel badge carried the message 'Founded in 1858'. However, research by the Society's publications committee revealed that it was a National Dahlia Show that was held in 1858. It was not until Christmas Eve, 1881 that a group of dahlia enthusiasts met in London and formed the National Dahlia Society, staging their first dahlia show in autumn 1882. Those who made up the new organization were moneyed gentry who delighted in competing against each other – although it was their gardeners who did the hard work! Right up to the years immediately before the last World War, entry cards for the National Show included a space for 'Gardener's Name'. Not many would be able to fill that in nowadays.

For the first 20 years or so of its existence the N.D.S. existed only for the shows. It was not until 1903 that one of the early Presidents, after some lengthy debate at committee meetings, uttered the now legendary phrase that 'the National Dahlia Society must popularize the dahlia throughout the length and breadth of the land . . . no matter for what purpose it shall be grown'. This statement of intent set the society on the course that it follows to this day, encouraging every type of dahlia and every interest, whether for exhibition, garden decoration or raising new varieties. After this, the first dahlia trials were grown at Dyffryn Castle, South Wales. Later, linking with the Royal Horticultural Society, their mentor and guide since the N.D.S. was formed in 1881, shows and trials were organised. In the early twenties, for example, the world-famed Wisley dahlia trials were started and remain as popular today as ever. The shows at the Royal Horticultural Society's Halls in Westminster, London, held during the last week of August or the first in September, have long been known as the finest all-dahlia shows in the world. A succession of visiting dahlia enthusiasts from the USA, the Antipodes and Europe would heartily confirm this. Unfortunately, a significant part of the Society's history, most of it from the early 1900s to the mid-twenties, was lost in a fire at the home of one of the Society's secretaries. But enough is known for us to piece together a continuing story of service to this unique flower.

MEMBERSHIP BOOM

Perhaps the best part of the N.D.S. history started with the membership explosion after the last War. There were only some 300 members on the Society's books at that time, a figure which had been fairly constant for two decades or more. But as people managed to obtain houses in the late forties, fifties and sixties, with a piece of ground to grow something for themselves, membership took off dramatically. When I took over as General Secretary in 1967, the membership was at its peak of some 7,500. Since those halcyon days, successive peaks and troughs of enthusiasm and not a few years of inflation have reduced the numbers to around 3,500, but despite such apparent slumps, the hard core's enthusiasm has never wavered. Once a dahliaman, always a dahliaman – or dahliawoman, as there are many skilled and successful ladies in our ranks.

It is beyond question that the National Dahlia Society performs a real service. They organize and manage the rules for judging at shows and the classification of all new varieties, by issuing the bi-annual *Classified Directory*. This booklet is a labour of love for the specially appointed committee charged with the responsibility for bringing some order to the otherwise obvious chaos that could result from a flower with so many disguises! Perhaps the most difficult task is the allocation of colour divisions. After all, colour is in the eye of the beholder, and what looks glowing bronze to one gardener could well be orange to another. However, after years of experience, the National Dahlia Society have 13 colour divisions: White; Yellow; Orange; Bronze; Flame; Red, Dark Red; Light Pink; Dark Pink; Lilac, Lavender or Mauve; Purples; Wines or Violets; Blends; Bi-Colours and Variegated.

Each of these main divisions is sub-divided to include more exact colourings, more descriptive than the simple word 'red', for instance, which can include variations like brick-red and beetroot red, and it has always been my view that if you are selecting a dahlia variety from a catalogue, then the earthy descriptions are the best because every gardener, without exception, knows the difference between brick-red and beetroot red! This chapter will have made it plain that the choice of dahlias available to gardeners of the eighties is quite bewildering. And such confusion, it has to be said, has been reduced by the National Dahlia Society's *Classified Directory*. After all, their committees would be the first to admit that not too many enthusiasts are interested in the narrow breakdown in sizes, unless of course there is an interest in exhibition. However, the formational analyses are of abiding interest to every gardener, whereby he or she is able to know whether a bloom will be of the Decorative form; Cactus or Semi-cactus types or of the more globular forms like the Ball and Pompon varieties.

In addition to these disseminations, the National Dahlia Society has introduced a unique system whereby information is recorded as to the ability (or otherwise) of the individual variety listed. Each inclusion is suffixed with one of three letters, E, G or C. These indicate value as a bloom for either Exhibition (E); Garden Use (G) or Cut flower (C). The information given is based on experience of the cultivation of the dahlias collated from the committee's opinions as well as being assessed against the lists of winning varieties (for those useful for exhibition) gathered from the Society's main shows, viz. those held annually at the Royal Horticultural Halls, Vincent Square, London and the northern event held in conjunction with the Harrogate Autumn Flower Show at that town's exhibition halls in North Yorkshire.

INFORMATION FOR THE SHOWMAN

If the *Classified Directory* created by the National Dahlia Society is a boon for the ordinary gardener, then it is also of inestimable value to the aspiring showman and to the exhibitor of long experience. Each section is clearly defined and separated by the essential size values that make up such an important part of dahlia shows. From the smallest division – the miniatures, to the very largest of all the exhibition dahlias, those termed as 'giants', all are neatly pigeon-holed accurately to avoid any confusion on the showbench. To obtain and be minutely accurate with such listings requires a great deal of study and many seasons' growing before any variety can be included. And when you consider that the results of these labours are used interna-

tionally to assist other national bodies to make their classifications, it can be appreciated just what a marvellous service is given voluntarily by these devoted horticulturists.

It would be unfair to mention the National Dahlia Society's work on behalf of classification without mention of the role played by the Royal Horticultural Society with whom the N.D.S. works hand in glove. Not only are the society's annual shows held at the R.H.S. headquarters in London's West End, but a great deal of the information gleaned comes from the famous dahlia trials held at the R.H.S. Garden, Wisley, Surrey every summer. To mount such a trial and to administer it effectively takes a great deal of organization, and this is achieved by electing half of the so-called Joint Dahlia Committee's members from the Royal Horticultural Society membership and the other half from the National Dahlia Society.

This latter committee, separate from the classification committee, meet on many occasions during the growing season to both select blooms for trial (in the following year of course) and to adjudicate on those that are already in cultivation. At the end of each season, the results are tabulated and then widely distributed by both societies via their separate literature. It goes without saying that the results from these expertly managed trials are highly sought after by gardeners all over the world, and for a nurseryman to be able to annotate a variety in his list with the words 'Awarded at Wisley Trials' is the crowning glory and virtually guarantees sales to his customers.

Judging examinations are held, and a list of some 400 qualified judges is available to any society in Britain. Their members are kept informed of dahlia news and lore by twice yearly publications, the *January Bulletin* and the widely acclaimed *Dahlia Annual*. Both go all over the world to the Society's wide international membership and to many overseas bodies like the American Dahlia Society, the Australian Dahlia Society and a similar body in New Zealand. Links are maintained through these international connections and any differences that exist, over classification, judging and so on, are amicably settled by the various representatives.

Conferences, society meetings and social events are held each year in the north and south and a second show, the Northern Dahlia Show, is held in conjunction with the prestigious Harrogate Great Autumn Show every September.

If you would like to become a member of the National Dahlia Society and learn more about this rewarding flower, why not contact the General Secretary, A. Winkless, 8 Station Road, Kirby Muxloe, Leicester, LE9 9EJ. The subscription is around £8 per annum.

Opposite: *'Salmon Symbol' is a typical example of the Semi-cactus form. A sport of famous 'Symbol', this one will certainly win prizes for you!*

INDEX

ACKNOWLEDGEMENTS

The publishers gratefully acknowledge the following photographers/agencies for granting permission to reproduce the colour photographs: Photos Horticultural Picture Library (pp. 12–13, 44, 48, 116–117); Harry Smith Horticultural Photographic Collection (pp. 16, 20–21, 25, 36, 40, 41, 49, 52, 53, 56, 64–65, 81, 84); Pat Brindley (pp. 32, 33, 80); and Philip Damp (pp. 45, 57, 60, 61, 73, 76, 85, 88, 92–93, 97, 105, 112, 113, 120). The photographs on pp. 28–29, 68, 69, 89, 101, 104 and 108–109 were taken by Bob Challinor.
All the line drawings are by Nils Solberg.
The publishers also gratefully acknowledge the Series Editor's contribution to the end of Chapter 2, p. 24, from the heading 'Combining dahlias with other plants'.